ALL ABOUT PERENNIALS

Written by
A. Cort Sinnes

Plant Selection Guide
written by
Michael D. McKinley

Edited by
Ken Burke

Graphic design by
John Williams
Barbara Ziller

Illustrations by
Cyndie Clark-Huegel

Ortho Books

Publisher
Robert L. Iacopi

Editorial Director
Min S. Yee

Managing Editors
Anne Coolman
Michael D. Smith
Sally W. Smith

Production Manager
Ernie S. Tasaki

Editors
Jim Beley
Susan Lammers
Deni Stein

Design Coordinator
Darcie S. Furlan

System Managers
Christopher Banks
Mark Zielinski

Photographic Director
Alan Copeland

Photographers
Laurie A. Black
Richard A. Christman

Production Editors
Linda Bouchard
Alice Mace
Kate O'Keeffe

Asst. System Manager
William F. Yusavage

Chief Copy Editor
Rebecca Pepper

Photo Editors
Anne Dickson-Pederson
Pam Peirce

National Sales Manager
Garry P. Wellman

Sales Associate
Susan B. Boyle

Operations Director
William T. Pletcher

Operations Assistant
Gail L. Davis

Administrative Assistant
Georgiann Wright

Address all inquiries to
Ortho Books
Chevron Chemical Company
Consumer Products Division
Box 5047
San Ramon, CA 94583

Chevron Chemical Company
6001 Bollinger Canyon Road, San Ramon, CA 94583

Acknowledgments

Manuscript consultants
Pamela J. Harper
Seaford, Virginia

George H. Scott
Arcadia, California

Carl A. Totemeier
Old Westbury Gardens
Old Westbury, New York

Photo sources
Arthur Hecht
San Rafael, California

The Bailey Arboretum
Oyster Bay, New York

Bluebird Nursery
Nebraska

Boerner Gardens
of Whitnall Park
Hales Corner, Wisconsin

Cantigny Estate
Wheaton, Illinois

The Case Estates of
Arnold Arboretum
Weston, Massachusetts

Charles Wilson
Joseph Harris Co., Inc.
Rochester, Illinois

The Chicago Botanic Garden
Chicago, Illinois

The Denver Botanic Garden
Denver, Colorado

Dick Turner
San Francisco, California

Dodge Freeman, Designer
Lake Forest, Illinois

Frank Cabot
Province of Quebec
Canada

Fred McGourty
Brooklyn Botanic Garden
Brooklyn, New York

Harold Epstein
Larchmont, New York

Jack Romine
Walnut Creek, California

Jane Gates
of the Helen Crocker Russell
Memorial Library of
Strybing Arboretum Society
Golden Gate Park
San Francisco, California

John Bryan
San Rafael, California

Sir John R. H. Thuron
Unionville, Pennsylvania

Judy Glattstein, Designer
Oyster Bay, New York

Longwood Gardens
Kennett Square, Pennsylvania

Marilyn Alimo, President
The Garden Clubs of Illinois

Oehme, Van Sweden
and Associates, Inc.
Washington, D.C.

Old Westbury Gardens
Old Westbury, New York

Paul Sibbitt
Novato, California

Peggy Keener
San Anselmo, California

Spring Hill Gardens
Mentor, Ohio

Wave Hill
Bronx, New York

Western Hills Nursery
Occidental, California

White Flower Farm
Litchfield, Connecticut

Photographers
(Names of photographers in alphabetical
order are followed by page numbers on
which their work appears. R = right,
C = center, L = left, T = top, and
B = bottom.)

William C. Aplin: 10B, 49R

John Blaustein: 8, 30, 33, 34

Josephine Coatsworth: 11, 13C,
16CL,BL, 19, 21T,B, 29, 31, 32, 36T, 40,
43B, 46, 48R, 55L, 58TL,BL, 59L, 60R

Derek Fell: 15, 55C, 56L, 62R, 63L, 64R,
65R, 66R, 68L, 69B, 70R, 71B, 73L, 75C,
83C, 84L,R, 85L, 89R, 93L, 94R

Pamela Harper: 1, 6–7, 12T, 13T,
16TL,TR, CR, 17T, 28, 38, 41, 50R, 51L,
56R, 57L, 59R, 65L, 67R, 68R, 69R,
70TL, 77R, 78R, 79L,R, 83L, 86TC,
86–87, 88L, 92R, 94L

Dmitri Kessel, Life Magazine, © 1980
Time, Inc.: 45T

Michael Landis: 36B, 57C, 58R, 66B

Michael McKinley: back cover, 4, 5, 9,
10T, 12R, 14, 16BR, 22, 23T,B, 24, 42T,
47, 49L, 52R, 53LR, 54R, 55R, 57R,
61T,B, 62L, 66TL, 69L, 70B, 71R, 72BLR,
73TR,BR, 74TL,BL, 75R, 76L,R, 77L,C,
78L, 80L, 81, 82L, 83R, 86BC, 87L, 88R,
90L,R, 91L,R,B, 93R

James McNair: 17B, 51R, 80R

Musée Marmottan, Institut de France,
Paris: 44T

National Portrait Gallery, London,
England: 42B, 43C

William Rockhill Nelson Gallery of Art,
Collection of Ralph T. Coe, "Garden at
Giverny" by Claude Monet: 44C

Ortho Photo Collection: 26, 45B

George Taloumis: 37, 50L, 51C, 52L, 54L,
63R, 64L, 67L, 80C, 85R, 86L, 92L

Tom Tracy: 71L

Stylist
Sara Slavin: 8, 30, 33, 34

Manuscript/Gardening Editor
Frank Shipe
San Francisco, California

Typography
Vera Allen Composition
Castro Valley, California

Color Separations
Color Tech Corp.
Redwood City, California

Front cover: Peonies

Back cover: Salmon-colored oriental
poppies and white and pink peonies
predominate in this border.

Title page: Magenta *Geranium
psilostemon* in the foreground with
Mimulas lewisii, middle right, combined
with old roses.

ALL ABOUT PERENNIALS

OLD-FASHIONED FAVORITES

Page 5. Perennial flowering plants have been included in gardens throughout history. They have stood the test of time, and as you will see in this book, they are still an important part of gardens today.

DESIGNING WITH PERENNIALS

Page 9. Perennials are frequently the framework of the garden. The principles of design, the planning steps, and the lists of plants for special purposes and conditions will help you design a garden, bed, or border just right for you.

FROM THE GROUND UP

Page 29. Learn how to start your own perennials or select the best transplants from nurseries, how to prepare the planting site, and how to plant and care for perennials. You'll find everything you need to know to grow vigorous perennials.

THE ART OF PERENNIAL GARDENING

Page 41. Like painting, when the design elements of color, texture, and form are carefully planned and balanced, a garden becomes a work of art. Here you will take a close look at gardens that can inspire any home gardener.

PLANT SELECTION GUIDE

Page 47. This guide includes descriptions, cultural requirements, and photographs of over one hundred of the most dependable and widely available perennials. Browse through this section for ideas and plants that please you.

OLD-FASHIONED FAVORITES

Many people find an old-fashioned appeal in perennial flowers; some use them for low-maintenance color; others make collecting and growing perennials into a life-long hobby. Any way you look at them, perennials mean beauty and pleasure to the gardener.

Above: The simple design of a formal garden provides a strong framework for profuse displays of perennial blossoms. Shown here is one of the classic gardens at Old Westbury Gardens in New York. Left: White hybrid lilies, black snake plant (*Cimicifuga racemosa*), and pink phlox stand out sharply against a shaded background, composing a picture of old-fashioned charm and perennial beauty.

For many people, perennials suggest images of old-fashioned gardens, the kind that "Grandma used to grow." In fact, they are old-fashioned, having been the favorites of many generations of gardeners. But they are also the favorites of many gardeners today, and for the same reasons as in the past: they are relatively easy to grow, last from year to year, and offer an abundance of flowers in an enormous array of colors and forms.

What distinguishes perennials from other plants? The best place to begin is by comparing them with annuals and biennials:

Annuals are plants that complete their entire life cycle in a year or less. In most cases, annuals are planted from seed in the spring, flower and set seed during the summer and early fall, and are killed by the first hard frosts of winter.

Biennials take two years to complete their life cycle. When grown from seed, the first year they produce leafy growth but no flowers; the second year they produce flowers, set seed, and die.

Perennials are plants that live more than two years. Many plants are perennial, including trees, shrubs, and bulbs; but the word as used commonly and in this book refers to perennial flowering plants that are *herbaceous*, meaning that their stems are soft and fleshy, not woody as with shrubs and trees. (Bulbs are classified separately because of their method of storing food.)

Woody shrubs and trees survive winters because their stems and trunks resist extreme cold. Herbaceous perennials survive varying degrees of winter cold by virtue of roots that are stronger and more vigorous than those of annuals and biennials. With the onset of cold, the tops of perennials die down but the roots remain alive in a dormant state, sending forth new foliage and flowers each year when the weather warms. If growing conditions are right, this pattern can continue for many years— some perennials, for example peonies, gas plant, bleeding heart, and hosta, have been known to outlive their owners.

This long life of the perennials presents the gardener with some outstanding advantages. Their continued presence in the garden saves the time, labor, and expense of replanting every year. In addition, it provides a kind of perpetual framework around which temporary plants can be placed. This lends a valuable coherence to the garden from one year to the next.

There are other advantages to perennials as well. Plants well adapted to your climate and planted in the right location will require very little attention. And since most perennials reproduce by sending out roots that generate new plants, they can provide you with vigorous new stock ready for transplanting.

Most intriguing for many gardeners is that perennials come in an astonishing profusion of form, color, shape, and size, and there are literally thousands of varieties available. This incredible diversity makes even the mere planning of a perennial garden an exciting and rewarding journey.

How to Use This Book

This book is both an idea book and a book of basic information. It contains ideas for combining and using perennials in many ways. But most importantly, it gives you the practical information you need to produce your own beautiful perennial garden.

If you are interested in planning a garden but are at a loss as to where to begin, read *Designing with Perennials*, beginning on page 9. This section will tell you everything you need to know to plan the garden that pleases you, from how to use perennials as spot plantings to actually laying out a plan for formal or informal beds or borders. You'll find valuable advice on choosing colors and how to mix them, and all the details you need to know to select your plants. We'll give you some solid guidelines on the trickiest aspect of perennial gardening—how to coordinate bloom cycles to achieve the effects you want. You'll also find information on the mixed perennial border and on an exciting new way to use perennials. In addition, you can learn about the cutting garden and perennials in containers.

For the information you need to grow the healthiest and most beautiful perennials, see *From the Ground Up*,

page 29. This section will tell you how to get your soil into excellent condition, where to find the best plants, and how to start your own from seed. You'll also find information on fertilizing, watering, mulching, and on pest and disease control.

For a leisurely tour through some exquisitely beautiful gardens of the past, see *The Art of Perennial Gardening*, starting on page 41. Some of these gardens, created by unusually gifted and famous gardeners, have profoundly influenced perennial gardening throughout the world, and continue to do so today. They may

serve as the inspiration you need.

And finally, the *Plant Selection Guide*, starting on page 47, is an invaluable reference for gardeners just beginning with perennials and for veterans as well. The guide lists more than one hundred different perennials commonly grown in the United States. To help you visualize your projected garden and learn to identify the plants, there are photographs of every entry. You'll also find the "hard facts" of culture, and more detailed information on problem areas and on special ways to get the best health and bloom from each plant.

Before You Begin

When you set out to create a beautiful garden there are many practical matters to be considered, especially in the vast world of perennials—the design of the garden, plant sources, all the cultural requirements, and much more. We hope to cover these matters, and we also hope that in addition to merely giving information, this book infects the reader with an enthusiasm, a spirit that goes beyond such practical considerations.

Gardeners can be among the most inspired and talented people when it comes to the task of creating a beautiful environment. The transformation of a bare plot of ground into a garden filled with colors, fragrance, the play of light and shadow, and the sound of birds and falling water can almost be seen as an act of magic.

In many cases the photographs in this book have caught that magic. By no means should you, as the reader, feel any hesitation about the desire to recreate, perhaps identically, some of the scenes presented on the following pages. They are meant as an inspiration, the inspiration for anyone to create their own special magic in the garden.

A true cottage garden defies reason and organization, but the results can be enchanting. The cottage garden style is an important key to many aspects of perennial gardening and is referred to frequently throughout this book. Included in the garden pictured above are pink lupines, old-fashioned climbing roses, blue delphiniums, and yellow Jerusalem sage (*Phlomius fraticosa*).

DESIGNING WITH PERENNIALS

Perennial flowering plants are an extremely versatile group. They are equally at home in any type of garden — from the formal perfection of a perennial border to the humblest of cottage gardens.

Above: An informal planting of yellow rudbeckias provides a welcome invitation for curious visitors to explore the rest of this garden; a good illustration of the fact that you don't need an abundance of perennials to create a desired effect. Left: The formal design of this perennial garden is softened by the use of grass pathways and vine-covered arches. Because formal gardens rely on simple geometry, they are often the easiest to design and install.

Perennials as a group are the most versatile of all plants in the landscape. There are perennials that thrive in every type of soil from wet to dry, fertile to infertile, and in every exposure from full sun to shade. You can plant them alongside streams or in the dappled shade of trees, and naturalize the more vigorous ones in meadows, in the "wild garden," or in problem areas such as hillsides, steep embankments, and rocky outcroppings.

If you have an established low-maintenance landscape of trees and shrubs and want to add some seasonal color to relieve the year-round sameness of the scene, perennials are the perfect way to do it without having to replant annuals every year. Many gardeners are surprised to find that adding even a few perennials to a dull landscape can transform it into an attractive garden.

Because perennials are long-lived

they are usually thought of as permanent plantings, but they needn't always be planted with permanence in mind. Like annuals they can be used as *temporary* fillers among shrubs and trees or to brighten up dull or vacant spots in the yard. Unlike annuals, however, if a time comes when they have to be removed, most can easily be transplanted elsewhere. It's possible, in fact, to use other parts of the yard as "holding areas" for perennials until time to plant them in the flower garden.

As versatile and effective as perennials are in difficult or unconventional situations, it is in the flower garden that they are truly outstanding. Year after year they can provide beautiful flowers and foliage over a long season, from early spring until late fall. They are solid, reliable plants, and the feeling of permanence and stability they bring to the garden in turn gives deep

Right: One of the cardinal rules of garden design is to situate the flower beds or borders so that they can be readily admired. The back porch of this house in Connecticut is a favorite sitting place, so the garden was arranged accordingly. Below: You don't need a multitude or diversity of perennials to create a big effect. A clump of daylilies enlivens an otherwise all-green landscape.

satisfaction and a welcome sense of security to every gardener.

Perennial gardening has been beloved throughout history, so much so that it has been developed, particularly in the form of the perennial border, into a genuine art. Later in this book we will see some examples of the glory the perennial border has reached through the efforts of some famous, extraordinarily skilled gardeners. In this section we will take a close look at the basic principles that led to these remarkable gardens, principles that will enable you better to understand and create your own beautiful gardens with perennials.

The Cottage Garden
The best place to begin learning to design a garden is with the garden that shows the least design of all: the cottage garden. It was the English cottage garden, using the same plants as its more formal counterparts, but without any particular plan or reason, that was the forerunner of the most beautifully designed perennial beds and borders.

Cottage gardens are essentially the gardens of people who love plants for themselves and care little or nothing for the way they are organized. Plants are added to the taste and at the whim of the gardener, and the only

guiding principle is to have close at hand all of those plants the gardener loves, without much regard for such rules as placing taller plants in back or leading up to bright colors with more subtle ones. The effect is likely to be kaleidoscopic, with an old climbing rose, a clump of daylilies, a mat of nasturtiums, a towering stand of hollyhocks, and spots of cottage pinks, basket-of-gold, veronica, poppies, and other plants all growing on their own, without much focus. They are gardens of surprises, where such accidents of nature as the encroaching of vigorous plants upon one another and the sudden appearance of plants the gardener doesn't recall planting are gratefully accepted. The true cottage garden has a wild and wooly look, but it is also a charming, engaging garden in which to lose oneself.

It may be that this loose approach to gardening and garden design appeals to you more than the idea of laying out a plan. Why, then, should you bother learning anything about design?

Why Design?
The simple fact is that gardens can have the same quantities of exactly the same plants, and some of these gardens will still be more attractive than others. In almost every case, the

difference is that the most beautiful gardens are those with a strong underlying design or structure. The sense of order a plan provides is especially important in flower gardens. With flowering plants, the variations in sizes, shapes, colors, and textures always pose the possibility of ending up with a messy jumble, and one that means more work. But if the basic framework of the garden is strong, any combination of plants and flowers can be supported easily, without the fear of chaos taking over.

Unfortunately, the planning stage is too often ignored by beginning gardeners. Their gardens tend to grow randomly, by bits and pieces, and if some order does emerge, it is more by luck than by conscious effort. In the long run, however, you will create a much more beautiful garden if you take time to draw up some type of overall plan. By the time your garden matures, this underlying design may not be as obvious as in the beginning, but the organization it provided will still be strongly felt.

Planning the Design

At the beginning of any truly successful garden, a thoughtful plan was devised and carried out. Such factors as the lawn size and shape, the paths and walkways, shrub borders, hedges, trees, statues, and background fences and walls all were considered, both individually and as contributors to the creation of a total scene.

There are basically five steps to designing the perennial garden:

• Determining the point from which the garden most often will be viewed.

• Considering the shape and topography of your yard and which plants are there that are immovable or that you want to keep.

• Deciding whether you want a formal or informal design.

• Deciding whether you want beds or borders.

• Choosing your plants.

The first step in planning your garden should be to determine from what angle or location it will most often be viewed. If you plan to view it primarily from inside the house, make sure to locate it so that you can see it comfortably through a favorite window. If you plan to spend a lot of time on a deck or patio, be careful to lay out the garden with that spot in mind.

Once you know where to place the garden, the next step is to consider the shape and topography of your yard. This will in turn help you to decide whether to have a formal or informal design.

Formal or Informal? If your yard is irregular, with slopes, hills, or rock

Pictured below is a traditional formal perennial garden. The stone walkway, flanked by identical wide beds, leads to a pergola-covered sitting area complete with sundial.

Left: If you have space for them, "island" flower beds are effective areas in which to grow perennials. Not only are they easy to maintain, but also they can be viewed from all sides. Below: Borders (areas accessible from one side only) can be used in both large and small gardens. Borders planted with a large number of diverse plants, such as the one below, should be as wide as they can be without making it difficult to tend the background plants.

outcroppings, or if there are mature trees or specimen plants that you wish to leave standing, you'll find it difficult to carry out a formal design. Such a site lends itself naturally to an informal plan, and most gardeners in these conditions will take that course. On the other hand, if your yard is flat with no outstanding natural features, you'll be free to choose whichever style you wish.

In the informal garden there is a predominance of curved flowing lines and a seeming disregard for symmetry. The curves of lawn areas, patios, walkways, beds, and borders are usually gentle, wide arcs frequently following the natural terrain. One curve should lead to another, creating a feeling of natural harmony.

Formal gardens are composed primarily of straight lines and classical symmetry; that is, what appears on the right side of the garden is matched, sometimes nearly perfectly, to the left. The outermost dimension of the formal garden is frequently rectangular, and this shape is repeated in other parts of the plan, in pools, patios, and in flower beds and borders. Often a single object such as a statue, pool, or sundial serves as the center of interest, placed for optimum effect usually toward the rear of the garden, directly in the line of vision from the favorite viewing spot.

A formal design is the easiest type of garden to lay out and because of its visual simplicity is usually the best choice for a small lot.

Once you have decided on the garden location and on a formal or informal plan, you want next to decide

whether to plant beds or borders (or both, if you have the space).

Beds and Borders. Beds and borders have been the key elements in garden design as long as there have been gardens. What are they exactly, and how do they differ? When we use the term "bed" in this book, we mean a cultivated area surrounded by an open expanse, usually a grass lawn. A border is a cultivated area that bounds or borders an expanse, such as ringing the perimeter of a lawn, and usually lies adjoining a walkway. Beds and borders may be designed along either informal or formal lines.

Beds For most of today's gardeners, the idea of a formal bed seems more at home in a public park or on municipal grounds than in one's own backyard. Indeed, in the home garden beds are generally less popular and practical than borders for the simple reason that they need fairly large open areas around them to look their best. Putting a bed into an average-size yard is like placing a table in the middle of an average-size room: it substantially cuts down the free space.

Still, beds have a number of important advantages. One strong proponent of informal beds, or "island beds," as he calls them, is Alan Bloom, one of the world's foremost authorities on perennials. Bloom favors beds for three reasons: first, because they are accessible from all sides they are easier to maintain than standard borders; second, they admit more sunlight and air circulation, which benefits plants; and third, because they can be viewed from all sides, they hold

more possibilities for the attractive arrangement of plants. If these features appeal to you and you have the space, beds may be ideal for your garden.

Borders The greatest advantage of the border over beds is that it allows more open space. If your yard is limited to the standard urban or suburban dimensions, there are good reasons for leaving the center open: to create the feeling of as much space as possible; to provide space for recreation; and to provide a "quiet" space to serve as contrast to whatever visual activity you may have on the perimeter of the yard—trees, shrubs, or the flower border itself.

Much of the effectiveness of the

border depends upon the open space it defines. There should be a pleasing relationship between the depth of the border (the distance from front to back) and the width of the yard. For example, if you want borders on each side of a yard 40 feet wide, borders 12 feet deep would create a "tunnel" effect. For a more pleasing proportion to the space borders enclose, their depth should never exceed more than a quarter of the total width of the yard.

In addition to allowing more open space, borders serve the unique purpose in any garden of softening the edges of buildings, fences, walkways, and lawns.

Borders are often installed so that they are flush against a building or fence and therefore accessible from one side only. This situation limits the border depth to about 5 feet; any deeper would make it difficult to tend plants in the back without walking on those in front. However, you can have a deeper border if you leave a space behind it at least 30 inches wide. The tallest plants will hide this rear path from view, but you will still be able to groom, prune, stake, and weed easily from that side. The path will also allow more of the air circulation plants need, and in addition make the border less vulnerable to invasion by the roots of shrubs or trees behind the border.

If you choose to plant a perennial border, you'll want to consider two other aspects of design: background and edging.

Backgrounds. For backgrounds, most of us must settle for whatver

serves currently to separate our property from adjacent properties. This most often is a fence or wall, but may also be a hedge, shrubs, or, in part, buildings.

No doubt the most attractive backdrop for a secluded garden is a stone or brick wall. Next best is a weathered, natural wood fence. If you have a fence painted or stained an unappealing or difficult color, keep in mind that if you repaint or restain, you may have to do it again every few years. Try to choose paint closest to the color of the wood in its weathered state. Medium-to-dark earth tones generally make the best backgrounds for flowers.

Top: An interesting design combination is found in the flower border that acts as an island bed. The shape of this planting space looks like a border, but because it juts out into the lawn area, it functions as a bed and can be tended from both sides. **Above:** Borders, more than beds, rely on the background to complete the garden picture. Some lucky gardeners can capitalize on the rustic qualities of a stone fence.

The edge of a flower bed or border is more important than the viewer often realizes. Many choices are available—from bricks to stones or wood. One strong point of a border is easy maintenance. In this border, which features lilies and perennial grasses, massive railroad ties separate the planting space from the gravel walkway.

If the fence is basically uninteresting, or if you have a chain link or wire fence or other structure that cannot serve as a backdrop, you can create a background by planting vines to make a tracery across the front. Wisteria, trumpet vine, lace vine, honeysuckle, and ivies are just a few possible choices.

Shrubs also make particularly attractive backgrounds. If you have room you may want to plant some, perhaps mixing evergreen and deciduous shrubs. Or you may want to plant a hedge. Needled evergreen hedges such as yew generally grow much more slowly than broadleaf hedge plants such as privet. They take fewer nutrients from the soil and are thus much slower to invade the border. If planted as small plants, however, they may take ten years or more to fill in completely. You may want to start with larger plants.

A list of tall perennials suitable for backgrounds appears on page 24.

Edgings. Edgings serve to set off beds and borders from the surrounding yard. They also can discourage or prevent lawn grass or weeds from creeping into the planted area.

If the bed or border fronts onto a lawn, a row of bricks laid side-by-side and set slightly lower than the level of the turf will not only define the planting area but make an excellent mowing strip. If your design is rectilinear, wood 2-by-4s or other lumber, even railroad ties, will make a strong edge. You will, however, have to edge the grass by hand where it meets the wood.

For a less formal look, fieldstones set in mortar can provide an attractive picture, especially if plants are allowed

to drape and trail over them. You can also simply line stones along the edge, if you wish. And if a walkway or lawn flanks the bed or border, many people choose to have the first row of plants grow into it in a natural manner, as seen in the photograph on page 15. A list of perennials for edging the border appears on page 24.

Another easy way to merely define the edge of a planting area is to install some of the small flexible wire fencing commonly available at garden centers.

Whatever you choose as your edging, remember that unless you provide some kind of underground barrier between the bed or border and the lawn, you'll be in for some extra weeding. Garden centers usually carry inexpensive rolls of metal or plastic strips for this purpose.

Choosing Plants

Once you have gone through the previous steps in designing your garden, you're ready for that part of gardening that most people find the most fun of all—choosing your own plants. As you begin to make those choices, you may find it helpful to ask yourself these important questions:

Are there any favorite plants that you "must have," or colors that you should not plant because they would clash with or be overwhelmed by the color of a background wall, fence, or planting?

Do you want one color scheme blooming all at once, or do you want a changing garden, with one wave of flowers giving way to the next?

Do you want a diversity of plant and flower forms, or plants that are more or less similar in appearance?

Does your space limit you to smaller

plants, or can you accommodate some of the rangier ones?

In designing the garden, there are several specific characteristics of perennials that you need to know in order to make the best choices. Obviously, the cultural requirements of the plants must match the soil, light, and climatic conditions in your garden. In addition, you need to note each plant's *color, height, spread, form, texture,* and *bloom season.* Let's look at each characteristic and the role it plays in garden design.

Color. Perennials come in a vast range of colors, so many that choosing can be confusing. However, some simple principles of color can help greatly in selecting your flowers and blending them in the garden.

The color wheel on this page is a device for showing the basic interrela-

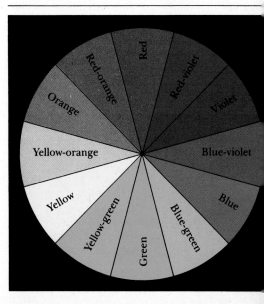

tionships of colors. For example, red, red-orange, orange, yellow-orange, and yellow are considered "warm"; green, blue-green, blue, blue-violet, and violet are considered "cool" colors. (Red-violet and yellow-green have both warm and cool properties, one more than the other depending upon what colors they are combined with.) Although colors are neither warm nor cool in a physical sense, they can impart *feelings* of warmth or coolness, and of passion or tranquility.

To the eye, warm colors tend to advance and cool colors tend to recede: if planted side-by-side at a distance, the warm colors would appear closer, the cool colors farther away. You can use these effects to create spatial illusions. A planting of predominantly cool-colored flowers at the rear of your garden would make the yard seem larger; warm colors would make it seem smaller. Spot plantings can have similar effects, seeming to deepen a part of the yard or to bring it closer.

Generally, cool colors are good for close-up viewing and warm colors better for dramatic displays. Plantings of blue campanula, violet meadow sage, and purple phlox may have quite an impact next to the patio or walkway, but planted in the background of the garden they would all but lose their effect. To emphasize cool colors, it's best to plant them closest to the point from which they'll be most often viewed. Warm-color plants such as red hibiscus, yellow heliopsis, and orange asclepias can be used to bring a distant part of the yard into sharp focus. When combining warm and cool colors, remember that the cooler colors can be easily overwhelmed by the warm.

A pure color is often called a *hue*. A *tint* is lighter than the pure color and a *shade* is darker. In combining hues, tints, and shades, there are four basic schemes:

Monochromatic schemes are those with flowers in various tints and shades of one color. No garden is truly monochromatic, of course, because the green of foliage is always present; but flowers in tints and shades of one color can be particularly harmonious and attractive, and the idea is certainly worth experimenting with. Many gardeners use this scheme to complement the color of the house.

Analogous schemes use colors closely related to one another on the color wheel. Any three adjoining colors are said to be analogous; for example, red, red-violet, and violet. These schemes have been used in creating some of the world's most beautiful gardens. On page 43 you will see the

famous "tonal" garden of Vita Sackville-West, based on rules quite similar to those for the analogous scheme.

Complementary schemes combine colors opposite one another on the wheel; for example, red and green, yellow and violet, and orange and blue. These are powerful combinations, clashing to some, vibrant and vital to others. They are best with pure hues, rather than shades or tints. If you want to try to "blend" strong complementary colors, arrange them to intermingle where they meet rather than be clearly defined. To tone these colors down you can include silvery-leaf or white-flower plants. If you want to plant intensely colored flowers like scarlet red Oriental poppies, clear yellow rudbeckias, or hot pink Michaelmas daisies, you can always lead up to the bright spots with plants of similar but less intense colors. Beds and borders designed along this

It is a fact of light that cool colors tend to recede and warm colors advance toward the viewer. An excellent example of this phenomenon is shown below. Note how the lavender-blue phlox fades into the background, while the darker blue delphiniums to the right are barely discernible against the shaded green hedge. The small clump of warm-orange lilies practically pops out of the scene, and the yellow-green gopher plant (*Alchemilla vulgaris*) has just enough yellow in it to make it stand out.

Several successful color combinations are shown in the photographs to the right. The top row features two monochromatic examples; the middle row, two analogous color schemes; and the bottom row, two complementary combinations. The flowers in each are listed.

Top left: red dahlias, red petunias, red tuberous begonias, and pelargoniums. The dark purple foliage in the background is smoke tree (*Cotinus coggygria* 'Notcutt's'). Top right: *Sedum spectabile* (foreground), *Monarda* 'Croftway Pink' (middleground), and pink cosmos (background).

Middle left: *Stachys officinalis* (foreground), sweet William and cosmos (middleground), and *Cirsium japonicum* (background). Middle right: achillea (foreground), helianthus (right), and rust-colored Helenium (background).

Bottom left: yellow *Aurinia saxatile* and purple *Scilla*. Bottom right: *Allium senescens* (bottom), yellow rudbeckia (left), and white *Achillea millefolium* 'Emerald Isle' (right).

principle have a pleasing rhythm and cohesion to them.

Polychromatic schemes often produce a gay, carnival-like atmosphere in the garden. They may combine any colors and every color. These are often the result of random plantings, particularly by the novice gardener. There is nothing wrong with this, assuming the gardener didn't have something else in mind, and in fact it can lead to some happy surprises—accidental but especially pleasing color combinations that become the mainstay of the garden for seasons to come.

These principles should be helpful in choosing flower colors for your garden. You'll find a list of perennials arranged by flower color on page 25. Foliage color is also a consideration. Perennials come with foliage in all shades and tints of green, in blue-green, blue-gray, silvery blue, silvery gray, gray, and in many variegations. Generally, it's a good idea when designing to avoid plants with variegated foliage. They are notoriously difficult to combine with flowers. Plants with silver or gray foliage, however, have been the pets of many gardeners. Dusty miller, santolina, lamb's ears, and verbascum are just some of the silver- or gray-foliage plants that have striking effects when combined with flowers, particularly white flowers or flowers in the pale blue to lavender range of the spectrum.

Height. Perennials range in height from under a foot to as much as 12 feet. The standard rule for borders is to stair-step the plantings from the tallest in the rear to the shortest in front. In island beds of mixed plantings, the tallest obviously should be toward the center. If these rules are followed strictly, however, the result is

likely to be too static a combination. Some variations in the rules will allow for a more natural effect and a more attractive garden, as long as plants aren't actually obscured from view. Lists of perennials arranged by height appear on page 24.

Spread. The spread of a plant at maturity is extremely important in garden planning and unfortunately is commonly overlooked by gardeners. Newly planted beds or borders, if planted with the correct spacings between plants, naturally look a little spare, more soil than plant. In the eagerness for a lush, full garden, the temptation is to fudge a little (or a lot) and space the young plants closer together than recommended. Although it may seem a nuisance to look up the spread of each plant and allow for it in your plan, rest assured that if you do not do it, you will eventually discover new meaning to the word "nuisance" by having to deal with a jammed-up formless jungle of plants most likely suffering from competing for light, water, and nutrients. If you do allow them enough room to grow, you'll be glad you did.

Form. Plants have their own forms, and these too are important design considerations. For all practical purposes, there are five basic forms in flowering plants: *rounded, vertical, open, upright and spreading,* and *pros-*

trate. Some gardens are composed of only one form; others alternate and repeat certain forms. Many outstanding beds and borders are made up of complementary forms, mixing the rounded with the vertical. If you have some difficulty in considering form for your design, it may help to imagine the garden in silhouette. Lists of perennials by form appear on page 24.

Although their characteristics are too subtle to play a great role in design, you may want to think about flower forms. The forms that perennial blooms take are too numerous and complex to enumerate, but some of them, and examples, are: the bell-shape campanulas, daisylike shasta daisies or asters, spherical peonies, cup-shape marsh marigolds, spurred columbines, frilly or lacy dianthus, star-shape amsonia, and trumpetlike daylilies. Flowers may also be borne singly at the ends of stems, in clusters, or in spikes.

The daisy family is so large that gardeners frequently find themselves with an overabundance of the daisy shape. Generally, the most interesting gardens are those that offer some contrast in flower forms.

Texture. When we speak of the texture of plants, we mean the textural *appearance* of the plant, not the way it feels to the touch. Plants may

Above: An excellent polychromatic color scheme is shown in the photograph above, taken at Healing Garden in England. The border is a skillful combination of plant forms and heights, foliage textures, flower shapes, and, last but not least, colors. Below: Silver- and gray-foliaged plants have a special appeal to many gardeners. Shown here are the low-growing gray lavender cotton (*Santolina chamaecyparissus*), the low-growing green pygmy barberry, and the taller gray lamb's ears (*Stachys olympica*).

Bloom Chart

	JAN	FEB	MAR	APRIL	MAY	JUNE	JULY	AUG	SEPT	OCT	NOV	DEC
Helleborus niger	■	■										
Helleborus lividus var. *corsicus*		■	■									
Helleborus orientalis			■	■								
Aurinia saxatilis				■	■							
Bergenia cordifolia				■	■							
Brunnera macrophylla				■	■							
Mertensia virginica				■	■							
Phlox subulata				■	■							
Primula vulgaris				■	■							
Primula × *polyantha*				■	■							
Primula sieboldii					■							
Pulmonaria saccharata				■	■							
Pulmonaria angustifolia				■	■							
Euphorbia epithymoides				■	■							
Iris, Bearded					■	■						
Aquilegia					■	■						
Caltha palustris				■	■							
Dianthus plumarius					■	■						
Doronicum cordatum				■	■							
Euphorbia cyparissus					■							
Geranium sanguineum					■	■						
Geum hybrids					■	■						
Iris, Pacific Coast					■	■						
Paeonia hybrids					■	■						
Polygonatum commutatum					■							
Primula japonica					■	■						
Stachys grandiflora					■	■						
Trollius europaeus					■	■						
Acanthus mollis						■						
Amsonia tabernaemontana					■	■						
Baptista australis					■	■						
Dicentra eximia					■	■	■					
Dicentra spectabilis					■	■						
Dictamnus albus					■	■						
Hemerocallis hybrids						■	■	■				
Alchemilla vulgaris					■	■						
Anchusa azurea						■	■					
Asclepias tuberosa						■	■					
Astilbe						■	■					
Campanula glomerata						■	■					
Campanula carpatica					■	■	■					
Chrysanthemum coccineum						■	■					
Chrysanthemum × *superbum*						■	■					
Coreopsis lanceolata						■	■	■				
Coreopsis verticillata						■	■	■				
Delphinium elatum						■	■					
Digitalis purpurea						■	■					
Filipendula hexapetala						■	■					
Gaillardia × *grandiflora*						■	■	■				
Arrhenatherum elatum (a grass)						■	■					
Heuchera sanguinea						■	■					
Kniphofia uvaria						■	■	■				
Lupinus 'Russell hybrids'						■	■					
Lychnis chaledonica						■	■					
Lychnis × *haageana*						■	■					
Lysimachia nummularia						■	■	■				
Lysimachia punctata						■	■					
Papaver orientalis						■						
Penstemon hartwegii						■	■					
Salvia pratensis						■	■					
Salvia × *superba*						■	■					
Scabiosa caucasica						■	■	■				

	JAN	FEB	MAR	APRIL	MAY	JUNE	JULY	AUG	SEPT	OCT	NOV	DEC
Thermopsis caroliniana						■	■					
Tradescantia virginiana						■	■					
Veronica incana						■	■					
Veronica latifolia						■	■					
Iris sibirica						■	■					
Achillea						■	■					
Aruncus dioicus						■	■					
Chrysogonum virginianum						■	■	■	■			
Cimicifuga racemosa							■	■				
Coreopsis grandiflora						■	■	■				
Filipendula rubra						■	■					
Filipendula ulmaria						■	■					
Deschampsia caespitosa (a grass)						■	■					
Iris kaempferi						■	■					
Monarda didyma						■	■					
Veronica hybrids						■	■					
Anthemis tinctoria						■	■					
Campanula persicifolia						■	■					
Chrysanthemum parthenium						■	■					
Echinacea purpurea							■	■				
Echinops exaltatus							■	■				
Euphorbia corollata							■	■				
Andropogon scoparius (a grass)							■	■	■	■	■	
Gypsophila						■	■					
Heliopsis helianthoides							■	■				
Hosta sieboldiana							■	■				
Hosta undulata							■	■				
Hosta ventricosa							■	■				
Liatris							■	■				
Lysimachia clethroides							■	■				
Lythrum salicaria							■	■				
Platycodon grandiflorus							■	■				
Stachys officinalis							■	■				
Stokesia laevis							■	■				
Thalictrum rochebrunianum							■	■				
Veronica longifolia							■	■				
Veronica spicata							■	■				
Belamcanda chinensis							■	■				
Helenium autumnale							■	■	■			
Hibiscus mosheutos							■	■				
Lobelia cardinalis							■	■				
Phlox paniculata							■	■	■			
Rudbeckia							■	■	■			
Salvia azurea							■	■				
Stachys byzantina							■	■				
Aconitum napellus								■	■			
Aster								■	■	■		
Ceratostigma plumbaginoides								■	■			
Chrysanthemum hybrids								■	■	■		
Cortaderia selloana (a grass)								■	■			
Molinia caerulea (a grass)								■	■			
Helianthus decapetalus								■	■			
Hosta fortunei								■	■			
Hosta decorata								■	■			
Hosta lancifolia								■	■			
Ligularia dentata								■	■			
Sedum spectabile								■	■			
Solidago hybrids								■	■			
Anemone × *hybrida*									■	■		
Miscanthus sinensis (a grass)									■	■		
Hosta plantaginea									■			
Hosta tardifolia									■	■		

be said to be *coarse, medium,* or *fine* in texture. Texture is determined by such factors as how dense the foliage is, the form of the plant, and how close the flowers are to one another. For example, the plume poppy is coarse in texture, the peony medium, and artemisia fine.

Like color, texture can be used to create spatial illusions in the garden. Coarse-textured plants will appear closer, and fine-textured plants will recede into the distance. This is useful, for example, with a long, narrow border. If you wish to make the far end seem closer, you can do so by planting coarse-textured plants at that end. Plants with a fine texture can make a shallow border appear deeper. A list of perennials especially valuable for textural effects can be found on page 27.

Bloom Season. And now we come to the most important single aspect of perennial gardening: timing bloom. To design with perennials you must know when each plant will bloom and for how long. Different perennials bloom at different times throughout the season and for different periods of time. (Some, of course, do coincide.) These factors must be coordinated to produce the effects you want. And this is the most challenging, most interesting, and most exciting feature of perennial gardening.

This coordination is necessary because, although there are many exceptions, perennials generally bloom for two to four weeks, a shorter duration than annuals, which generally bloom throughout the season. To extend color over time, you must select plants with varying blossoming times or durations of bloom. (If faded flowers are cut back, most perennials will bloom again. This second bloom will produce more, but smaller flowers.)

Of course, you may want to select flowers that do bloom at approximately the same time for a garden filled with color. This is fine if you want a spectacular display and are willing to settle for little or no perennial bloom the rest of the season. Or you may want a longer duration of color and plant for a continuous succession of bloom, with new flowers appearing as others fade. This will have a diluting effect on the overall garden color; but it will also reveal something more of the forms of the plants. In general, even when you plant for a succession of bloom, there will be three or four peak periods of bloom during the season, interspersed with periods of quietude.

While it may be difficult to envision these changing patterns, a time lapse film of a perennial border taken from early spring to late summer would clearly show one wave of flowers re-

placing another. We can't show you that film, but on pages 22 and 23 is an excellent example in pictures of how a perennial garden changes through the growing season.

To help you pick perennials for a succession of bloom, the chart on page 18 illustrates how they relate to one another in blossoming time and duration of bloom season.

With the varying blossoming times and duration of bloom, the possibilities of the perennial garden are immense. When you add the job of coordinating color to coordinating these two factors, the possibilities become even more immense, so great that they may intimidate the beginning gardener. The question might be raised, why bother with all this, why not merely plant annuals for a full season of bloom? The simple answer, apart from the uniquely attractive characteristics and longer life of the perennials, is that the perennial garden planned for a succession of bloom is always changing, and in this is not one garden, but many gardens in one.

The Plant Selection Guide starting on page 47 is an ideal way to find out a great deal about many different perennials in a short time. It lists all of the previously mentioned characteristics—cultural requirements, color, height, spread, form, texture, and bloom season—for each plant. The lists beginning on page 24 will help you choose plants for different characteristics and cultural conditions. You'll find additional sources for plants and plant information on page 27. As you learn more about the individual plants, it's good to keep a list of those you think may be good for your garden, so that you'll have it handy when you begin laying out your plan on paper. See page 20 for two sample plans.

Mapping the Garden
Assuming you have gone over the design basics and have chosen or are in the process of choosing your plants, you may be ready to start drawing up a garden plan.

Graph paper will allow you to get the most realistic picture of your space and proportions. It is easy to work with paper with four squares to the inch, allowing each square to represent one square foot of garden space.

First, outline on the paper the shapes of your beds and borders. Then from a numbered list of your plant choices, insert the numbers on your plan. If you wish, you can insert information on any of the plant characteristics, whatever might give you a better picture of the garden. You can use any designations you want for these characteristics; for example, *T, M,* and *S* (for tall, me-

Some of the best flower gardens include a mixture of annuals, perennials, shrubs, herbs, and many other plants. Shown here is a pleasing combination of annual pansies and pink dianthus.

dium, or short) might be used for height; *CT, MT,* or *FT* might be used for coarse, medium, and fine texture. Some gardeners find it helpful to use colored pencils to indicate color. And if you are planning for a succession of bloom, you can use overlaying layers of tracing paper to indicate how the garden will appear at different times of the year.

Your plan can be as simple or complex as you like, and you can draw as many as you like. When you happen upon a scheme you prefer, you'll know it.

The Mixed Border
When you choose plants for the perennial border, by no means are you limited to perennials entirely. In fact, if what you aspire to is a fairly steady blaze of color, you'll have to add other plants, because this can't be provided by perennials alone.

Perennials do have the advantage of being permanent additions to the border, and thus provide the basic framework; but for the most part the warm-season annual flowers have a longer season of bloom. This makes them indispensable for color during "quiet" periods in the garden or to succeed faded perennial bloom.

Many of the most beautiful flower beds and borders in the world have predominately perennial plants, but annuals, bulbs, flowering shrubs, and many other plants are equally important parts of the scene. If you limit yourself to perennials alone, you'll miss out on such powerful color combinations as pink coral bells and orange California poppies, orange nasturtiums and blue salvia, and rich purple

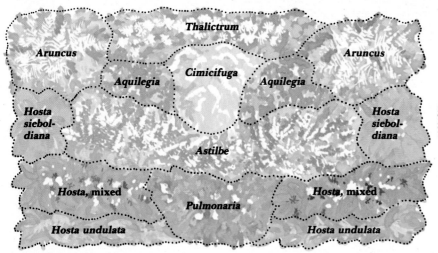

Thalictrum

Aruncus · Cimicifuga · Aruncus

Aquilegia · Aquilegia

Hosta sieboldiana · Hosta sieboldiana

Astilbe

Hosta, mixed · Hosta, mixed

Pulmonaria

Hosta undulata · Hosta undulata

Left: Subtlety is the key intention of this border plan. Below: Sequence of bloom is the key to this border.

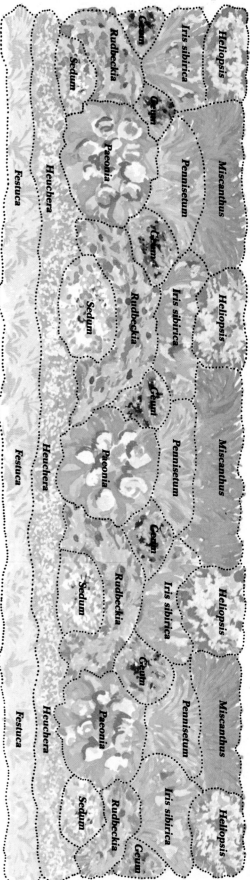

Sedum · Rudbeckia · Geum · Iris sibirica · Heliopsis

Festuca · Heuchera · Paeonia · Geum · Pennisetum · Miscanthus

Sedum · Rudbeckia · Iris sibirica · Heliopsis

Geum

Paeonia · Pennisetum · Miscanthus

Festuca · Heuchera · Sedum · Rudbeckia · Iris sibirica · Heliopsis

Geum

Paeonia · Pennisetum · Miscanthus

Festuca · Heuchera · Sedum · Rudbeckia · Iris sibirica · Heliopsis

Geum

A Textural Border for a Shady Spot

The border above is designed for a moist, shady area. The plants in it were chosen for their understated qualities of foliage and texture or their ability to accentuate those qualities. Form and color of foliage and flower shape may play an even more effective role than flower color, which serves primarily as accent.

In zone 6, flower color will be most apparent from late June to early July, with the exception of the early-blooming *Pulmonaria* and *Aquilegia*. *Astilbe, Aruncus, Cimicifuga,* and *Thalictrum* blossoms lend a feathery texture to the border. *Astilbe, Cimicifuga,* and *Hosta* add a spikey quality.

The play of foliage against foliage enlivens the garden in all seasons. *Cimicifuga, Astilbe,* and *Aruncus* echo one another in the similarity of their complicated, compound leaves, with textures ranging from medium to bold.

The simple variegated and various-colored cabbagelike leaves of *Hosta* and *Pulmonaria* range from gray to light and dark green, in medium to very bold textures.

Both *Aquilegia* and *Thalictrum* have fine, soft-textured, grayish foliage resembling maidenhair fern.

Plant List. The number in brackets following each entry is the number of plants you will need for this 6-by-10-foot border.
Aquilegia (Columbine); mixed blue, yellow, pink [4]
Aruncus dioicus (Goatsbeard); white [2]
Astilbe hybrids (False Spirea); whites and pinks [10]
Cimicifuga racemosa (Bugbane); white [4]
Hosta, mixed
    H. Plantaginea (Fragrant Plantain Lily); white [4]
    H. lancifolia (Narrow-Leaf Plantain Lily); pale lilac [4]
    H. ventricosa (Blue Plantain Lily); pale lilac [4]
Hosta sieboldiana (Blue-Leaf Plantain Lily); pale lilac [2]
Hosta undulata (Wavy-Leaf Plantain Lily); pale violet [8]
Pulmonaria saccharata (Bethlehem Sage); blue, reddish violet [5]
Thalictrum rochebrunianum (Lavender Mist Meadowrue); lavender [4]

A Garden That Changes with the Season

The border plan on the right offers change and progression, from bulbs and peonies through summer blossoms and winter grasses. *Festuca* and *Heuchera* provide an evergreen edging. The other plants, including peonies and iris, display good foliage during all growing seasons.

In May, the peonies blossom. Their flowering overlaps that of the Siberian irises, which peak in June along with the *Heuchera*, as the *Geum* and *Heliopsis* begin to flower.

Geum and *Heliopsis,* with long flowering seasons from late June through August, share the garden with *Rudbeckia,* which peaks in late July and into August, and *Sedum,* which blooms in August.

By early July, the grasses have gained good height. They flower, then seed in mid-August and into winter. Their seeds and foliage color and that of *Rudbeckia* and *Sedum* provide interest until spring.

Except for *Heliopsis* and *Festuca,* which perform best with yearly division, the plants in this garden require low maintenance.

For unity and added color, fragrance, and texture, underplant with long-lived bulbs, such as narcissus, and seed in forget-me-nots.

Plant List. The number in brackets following each entry is the number of plants you will need for this 6-by-20-foot border.
Festuca ovina 'Glauca' (Blue Fescue); silvery blue, evergreen foliage [54]
Geum 'Mrs Bradshaw' (Avens); red [7]
Grasses: *Miscanthus sinensis* 'Gracillimus' (Eulalia Grass); pinkish or silvery plumes [10]
    Pennisetum alopecoroides (Fountain Grass); coppery tan flowers [6]
Heliopsis helianthoides (Heliopsis); yellow [8]
Heuchera sanguinea (Coral Bells); pinks and whites [50]
Iris sibirica (Siberian Iris); blue [12]
Paeonia hybrids (Peony); pinks and whites [5]
Rudbeckia fulgida 'Goldsturm' (Goldsturm Black-eyed Susan); yellow with black [10]
Sedum spectabile (Showy Sedum); pinks and whites [14]

heliotrope with dark rose penstemon.

Spring- and summer-flowering bulbs are also important to any flower border, if only for the variety of unusual flower shapes they provide: daffodils in many varieties, grape hyacinths, fritillaria, tulips, and crocus are just a few of the spring-blooming bulbs that add excitement to the border well in advance of most perennial and annual bloom. The midsummer border can be made more interesting by adding any of the lily hybrids, the cactus-flowered dahlias, nerine, gladiolus, and the many varieties of allium.

The main drawback to an all-perennial border is that it is bare in winter. If you include a few hardy shrubs or small trees, you'll have something to look at during the cold months to testify that there is indeed a garden under all that snow or rain-soaked earth. When choosing shrubs and small trees for the border, it's best to pick those that will not overgrow their allotted space; and to look for varieties with some interesting fall or winter characteristics, such as bright foliage, berries, or an attractive branch pattern when the plant is bare. Such trees include dwarf forms of crabapple or flowering cherry, Japanese maple, or the flowering chestnut. Dwarf hollies, the tree peonies, dwarf junipers, and varieties of hebe are only a few of the shrubs that are restrained in growth.

The Cutting Garden
If you're a person who enjoys bringing the beauty of cut flowers indoors, you may want to consider setting aside a small bed primarily for an old-fashioned cutting garden.

Perennial flowers are among the most prized of all cut flowers, lending themselves particularly to large bouquets of striking impact. A dozen or so red-hot pokers in a tall glass cylinder, masses of blue delphiniums in a copper kettle, or a combination of sunflowers and coreopsis in a rustic wicker container are just a few possibilities.

Because the cutting garden is basically utilitarian, it should be laid out in a simple, practical manner. The plants can be planted in rows like a vegetable garden, with the tallest set so they won't shade the lower-growing varieties. A seldom-used sideyard is an ideal place for a cutting garden as long as it receives at least a half day of sun. The soil should, of course, be properly prepared.

Cut flowers will keep longer if you follow a few simple rules. Generally, it's best to cut flowers in the morning or evening when they are most turgid with water; flowers cut in the middle of the day are somewhat wilted and

once cut will have difficulty absorbing enough water.

Always use a sharp knife or pair of scissors to make the cleanest cut possible. Take a bucket or pail of warm water into the garden and plunge the stems into it immediately after they have been cut.

When arranging the flowers remove any foliage from the base of the stems to discourage the water in the vase from quickly spoiling. Professional flower arrangers often cut the stems again before putting the flowers into the vase. For the longest life, they advise cutting stems underwater and making the cut at an angle.

Place the arrangements in a cool room away from direct sunlight, and change the water daily, to promote the longest life. Cut flower "foods" available at some garden centers and florists can be added to the water to prolong the blossoms.

Cutting gardens also serve as excellent places to hold perennials in reserve until you want to plant them in the landscape or garden.

A list of perennials that make outstanding cut flowers can be found on page 27.

Perennials in Containers
Perennials can make excellent container plants, especially when combined with annuals or bulbs. Such plantings provide a much longer season of color and a good contrast between foliage and flowers. As the early bulbs and perennials pass their prime, the annuals can fill in and cover with a summer-long display of flowers.

Some combinations with annuals, perennials, and bulbs that you might want to try are: dark pink penstemons and a lighter pink 'Cascade' petunia; perennial blue salvia with blue trailing lobelia; 'King Alfred' daffodils with

Top: A cutting garden separate from the rest of the yard can provide plenty of flowers for indoor use. The owner of this cutting garden specializes in long-stemmed chrysanthemums. Above: An unusual container planting includes statice, ivy geranium, and ivy.

basket-of-gold; and the bushy Connecticut Yankee' delphinium, blue hyacinths, white sweet alyssum, and 'Blue Mariner' petunias.

Container Culture. From a design point of view, containers offer the advantage of mobility. You can group containers around the patio or deck or about an entryway, adding color where you like and changing the color schemes and patterns as you wish. Containers also can serve as holding areas for flowers you may wish to plant later in the garden.

Garden centers, nurseries, and variety stores offer wide selections of containers in all sizes: clay and ceramic pots, wooden half-barrels, and plastic and wood pots and boxes. Experienced container gardeners favor the largest containers possible: the bigger they are, the more soil they hold, which means less watering for the gardener, more root space for the plants, and more room to experiment with different combinations of plants.

If you use clay pots, it's a good idea to wet them down thoroughly before planting. Clay is very porous and if dry will quickly rob newly planted plants of their first soaking. Cover the drainage hole (or holes) with broken pieces of pottery, irregularly shaped stones, or a small piece of fine-mesh screen. (It is not necessary to provide additional drainage with a layer of gravel or stones on the bottom.)

You can fill the containers with garden soil *if* your soil is a good loam with excellent drainage. If you've had problems growing plants in your soil, you'll only intensify the problems when you use it in containers. Repeated waterings tend to compact soil to the point where there is very little air space left, making drainage very slow. If your soil is marginally acceptable, mix it in equal proportions with an organic soil amendment such as peat moss, compost, or redwood soil conditioner, to make it a lighter, looser growing medium more conducive to growing plants in confined quarters. If your soil is actually poor, you'll be better off using one of the prepackaged soil mixes sold under a variety of brand names such as Jiffy Mix, Redi-Earth, Metro Mix, Super Soil, Pro-Mix, and many others.

Before planting, thoroughly water the soil mass and allow it to settle. After settling, the soil should be 2 to 3 inches below the container rim. There should be enough space between the rim and the soil so that *one* watering will moisten the rootball and drain through. If the container is too full of soil, the job becomes time-consuming and aggravating, requiring several waterings for a complete soaking.

Because of the limited amount of soil available, plants in containers need more attention than plants in the open ground. During the hot summer months, daily watering is commonly needed, especially if the containers are in a sunny or windy location. These repeated waterings leach nutrients out of the soil rather quickly. To compensate for this loss, most container gardeners favor applying liquid balanced fertilizers at half-strength every two weeks.

To keep specimens looking their best, be sure to pinch off any dead flowers or leaves regularly.

A New Look for Perennials

It's often said that there is nothing really new in gardening; and it is certainly true that most new trends in gardening tend to be a revival of some sort, a rediscovery of a form of gardening from the past. In recent years, though the landscape architecture firm of Oehme, van Sweden & Associates in Washington, D.C., has designed a number of dramatic gardens, the likes of which have not been seen before. The plants are certainly not new, but the way they are being used and the aesthetics behind the garden design are fresh and different enough to constitute a new form of gardening.

The governing concept behind these gardens is the creation of a low-maintenance landscape using masses of a limited number of different plants, the majority of which are perennials. But they don't resemble anything like the English perennial border—rather than emphasizing flower combinations, these gardens are carefully thought out displays of contrasting textures and forms, with a subtle use of color that changes constantly with the seasons.

A garden by Oehme, van Sweden & Associates might start out in early spring with a massive display of naturalized daffodils or grape hyacinths, all bulbs that can remain undisturbed for years and which multiply in the process. These are followed in early summer by the lush new growth of black-eyed Susans (*Rudbeckia hirta*), *Sedum spectabile*, fountain grass (*Pennisetum setaceum*), elatia grass (*Micanthus sinesisis* 'Gracillimus'), and plume pop-

Left: Two photographs of the same garden, designed by Oehme, van Sweden & Associates, show the garden in early summer and late fall. The primary plantings are *Sedum spectabile,* fountain grass, plume poppies, and pampas grass. Equally beautiful in both seasons, this type of landscaping represents a new trend in gardening with perennials. Below: Another garden by Oehme, van Sweden & Associates was photographed in mid-summer. Although most of the grasses have not begun to flower, the large bed of black-eyed Susans creates a powerful impact.

pies (*Macleaya* species). In midsummer the black-eyed Susans begin to bloom in what can only be described as a huge outdoor bouquet (see the illustration), followed shortly by the plume poppies. In late summer the grasses start to send up their feathery plumes, followed by the flowering sedum. The sedum flowers start out pale greenish-white and, as the weather turns progressively cold, change from pink to a deep dusky rose.

Instead of trimming off all the spent flowers and dried leaves, the architects leave the plants intact through the first hard frosts and snow. What remain are the dried leaves of the grasses, with their tall, bare seed spikes, the dark seed heads of the black-eyed Susans, and the by now bronze flowers of the sedum, just before they disappear under a blanket of snow. One of the principals in the firm says the winter garden looks like an oversize dried arrangement of flowers and leaves.

These unique gardens dramatically illustrate the extraordinary creative possibilities in designing with perennials.

The feathery textured flowers of *Astilbe* and the spikey quality of *Hosta* work together to make form as important as color in this garden.

Perennial Performers

The following lists of perennials are categorized by plant height, form, color, application to special problems, and use. The lists can be an invaluable tool for the gardener who needs to organize many different elements into a cohesive whole. Use them to spark your imagination or to solve landscaping problems. Keep in mind that, in many cases, when a name appears on a list, only selected varieties (usually too numerous to mention in the list) may fit the given category. Consult the Plant Selection Guide, seed catalogs, and local experts to help pinpoint the variety most suited to your needs.

Low Perennials

Low perennial plants grow to no more than 18 inches in height and are useful in the front of a border, for edging, or in front of taller, leggy plants. Those marked with an asterisk (*) have the additional quality of spreading by forming mats or trailing across the ground and are useful in beds or as groundcovers.

Achillea ptarmica (Yarrow)
* *Alchemilla* (Lady's Mantle)
* *Armeria* (Sea Pink)
Artemisia (Wormwood)
Aster, selected varieties (Aster)
* *Astilbe* (False Spirea)
* *Aurinia* (Basket-of-Gold)
* *Bergenia* (Bergenia)
* *Brunnera* (Siberian Bugloss)
Campanula carpatica (Carpathian Harebell)
* *Ceratostigma* (Blue Plumbago)
Chrysanthemum hybrids, selected varieties (Hardy Chrysanthemum)
Chrysanthemum parthenium (Feverfew)
* *Chrysogonum* (Golden Star)

Large Perennials

Large perennial plants provide a general effect of mass with their dense foliage serving as backdrop to a border. An asterisk (*) indicates that the plant may reach a height of 5 feet or more.

Aruncus dioicus (Goatsbeard)
Baptisia australis (False Indigo)
Delphinium elatum (Delphinium)
Grasses: *Andropogon scoparius*
　　　　(Little Bluestem)
　　　　Cortaderia selloana
　　　　(Pampas Grass)*
　　　　Miscanthus sinensis
　　　　(Eulalia Grass)*
Helianthus decapetalus (Sunflower)
* *Hibiscus moscheutos* (Rose Mallow)
Thalictrum rochebrunianum (Lavender Mist Meadowrue)
Thermopsis caroliniana (False Lupine)

* *Dianthus* (Pink)
Gaillardia (Blanket Flower)
Geranium (Cranesbill)
Grasses: *Elymus* (Blue Lyme Grass)*
　　　　Festuca (Blue Fescue)
　　　　*Hakonechloa**
* *Gypsophila repens* (Creeping Baby's Breath)
* *Heuchera* (Coral Bells)
* *Hosta* (Plantain Lily)
* *Iris,* dwarf bearded (Dwarf Bearded Iris)
* *Lysimachia nummularia* (Moneywort)
* *Phlox subulata* (Moss Pink)
* *Primula* (Primrose)
* *Pulmonaria* (Lungwort)
Sedum (Stonecrop)
* *Stachys byzantina* (Wooly Betony)
Trollius (Globe Flower)

Form: Vertical Accent

The plants listed include those with an overall vertical form and with spikey or nonspikey flowers, and those with only spikey flowers.

Acanthus (Bear's Breech)
Astilbe (False Spirea)
Baptisia (False Indigo)
Cimicifuga (Bugbane)
Delphinium (Delphinium)
Digitalis (Foxglove)
Grasses: *Andropogon* (Little Bluestem)
　　　　Cortaderia (Pampas Grass)
　　　　Miscanthus (Eulalia Grass)
Iris (Iris)
Kniphofia (Torch Lily)
Liatris (Blazing Star)
Ligularia dentata 'The Rocket' (Golden Groundsel)
Lobelia cardinalis (Cardinal Flower)
Lupinus (Lupine)
Penstemon (Beardtongue)
Primula japonica (Japanese Primrose)
Salvia (Sage)
Stachys grandiflora (Big Betony)
Thermopsis (False Lupine)
Veronica (Speedwell)

Form: Rounded

The following plants have a smoothly rounded, bushy habit of growth and are dense, in general, with foliage from top to bottom.

Artemisia (Wormwood)
Aruncus (Goatsbeard)
Baptisia (False Indigo)
Chrysanthemum parthenium (Feverfew)
Chrysanthemum × superbum (Shasta Daisy)
Coreopsis verticillata (Threadleaf Coreopsis)
Dicentra (Bleeding Heart)
Dictamnus (Gas Plant)
Euphorbia (Spurge)
Gaillardia (Blanket Flower)
Geranium (Cranesbill)
Grasses: *Deschampsia* (Tufted Hair Grass)
      Helictotrichon (Blue Oat Grass)
      Festuca (Blue Fescue)
Gypsophila (Baby's Breath)
Helenium (Sneezeweed)
Heliopsis (Heliopsis)
Hemerocallis (Daylily)
Hosta (Plantain Lily)
Paeonia (Peony)
Sedum spectabile (Showy Stonecrop)
Thermopsis (False Lupine)

Form: Open

The plants in this list have an open, loose form. They are best displayed when mixed and interplanted with other perennials in a border.

Aquilegia (Columbine)
Echinacea (Coneflower)
Echinops (Globe Thistle)
Helianthus (Sunflower)
Lychnis coronaria (Rose Campion)
Papaver (Poppy)
Scabiosa (Pincushion Flower)
Thalictrum (Meadowrue)
Tradescantia (Spiderwort)

Flower Color: The Yellow Range

These plants include varieties with flowers in the color range from yellow-green and yellow to orange and bronze.

Achillea (Yarrow)
Alchemilla (Lady's Mantle)
Anthemis (Golden Marguerite)
Aquilegia (Columbine)
Asclepias (Butterfly Flower)
Aurinia (Basket-of-Gold)
Caltha (Marsh Marigold)
Chrysanthemum (Chrysanthemum)
Coreopsis (Calliopsis)
Delphinium (Delphinium)
Digitalis (Foxglove)
Doronicum (Leopard's Bane)
Euphorbia (Spurge)
Gaillardia (Blanket Flower)
Geum (Avens)
Helenium (Sneezeweed)
Helianthus (Sunflower)
Heliopsis (Heliopsis)
Helleborus (Christmas Rose)
Hemerocallis (Daylily)
Iris (Iris)
Kniphofia (Torch Lily)
Ligularia (Groundsel)
Lupinus (Lupine)
Lychnis (Campion)
Lysimachia nummularia (Moneywort)
Lysimachia punctata (Yellow Loosestrife)
Paeonia (Peony)

Papaver (Poppy)
Penstemon (Beardtongue)
Primula (Primrose)
Rudbeckia (Black-eyed Susan)
Solidago (Goldenrod)
Thermopsis (False Lupine)
Tradescantia (Spiderwort)
Trollius (Globe Flower)

Flower Color: The Whites

These plants include varieties with flowers in the color range from white to cream.

Acanthus mollis (Bear's Breech)
Achillea ptarmica (Yarrow)
Anthemis (Golden Marguerite)
Aquilegia (Columbine)
Armeria (Sea Pink)
Aruncus (Goatsbeard)
Aster (Aster)
Astilbe (False Spirea)
Bergenia (Bergenia)
Campanula (Harebell)
Chrysanthemum (Chrysanthemum)
Cimicifuga (Bugbane)
Delphinium (Delphinium)
Dianthus (Pink)
Dicentra (Bleeding Heart)
Dictamnus (Gas Plant)
Digitalis (Foxglove)
Echinacea (Coneflower)
Filipendula (Queen of the Prairie)
Geranium (Cranesbill)
Gypsophila (Baby's Breath)
Hemerocallis (Daylily)
Heuchera (Coral Bells)
Hibiscus (Rose Mallow)
Hosta (Plantain Lily)
Iris (Iris)
Kniphofia (Torch Lily)
Liatris (Blazing Star)
Lupinus (Lupine)
Lysimachia clethroides (Gooseneck Loosestrife)
Monarda (Bee Balm)
Paeonia (Peony)
Papaver (Poppy)
Penstemon (Beardtongue)
Phlox (Phlox)
Polygonatum (Solomon's Seal)
Primula (Primrose)
Stokesia (Stokes' Aster)
Thalictrum (Meadowrue)
Tradescantia (Spiderwort)
Veronica (Speedwell)

Flower Color: The Red Range

These plants include varieties with flowers in the color range from red to pink and pinkish-purple.

Achillea millefolium 'Fire King' (Fire King Yarrow)
Aquilegia (Columbine)
Armeria (Sea Pink)
Aster (Aster)
Astilbe (False Spirea)
Bergenia (Bergenia)
Campanula (Harebell)
Chrysanthemum coccineum (Painted Daisy)
Chrysanthemum hybrids (Hardy Chrysanthemum)
Delphinium (Delphinium)
Dianthus (Pink)
Dicentra (Bleeding Heart)
Dictamnus albus var. *purpureus* (Rose Gas Plant)
Digitalis (Foxglove)

Filipendula (Queen of the Prairie)
Gaillardia (Blanket Flower)
Geranium (Cranesbill)
Geum (Avens)
Grasses: *Cortaderia* (Pampas Grass)
      Pennisetum (Fountain Grass)
Gypsophila (Baby's Breath)
Helleborus (Christmas Rose)
Hemerocallis (Daylily)
Heuchera (Coral Bells)
Hibiscus (Rose Mallow)
Iris (Iris)
Kniphofia (Torch Lily)
Liatris (Blazing Star)
Lobelia (Cardinal Flower)
Lupinus (Lupine)
Lychnis (Campion)
Lythrum (Purple Loosestrife)
Monarda (Bee Balm)
Paeonia (Peony)
Papaver (Poppy)
Penstemon (Beardtongue)
Phlox (Phlox)
Platycodon (Balloon Flower)
Primula (Primrose)
Pulmonaria (Lungwort)
Scabiosa (Pincushion Flower)
Sedum (Stonecrop)
Thalictrum (Meadowrue)
Tradescantia (Spiderwort)
Veronica (Speedwell)

Flower Color: The Blue Range

These plants include varieties with flowers in the color range from blue and violet to lavender and bluish-purple.

Amsonia (Blue Star)
Anchusa (Bugloss)
Aster (Aster)
Baptisia (False Indigo)
Brunnera (Siberian Bugloss)
Campanula (Harebell)
Ceratostigma (Blue Plumbago)
Delphinium (Delphinium)
Echinacea (Coneflower)
Echinops (Globe Thistle)
Geranium (Cranesbill)
Hosta, selected species (Plantain Lily)
Iris (Iris)
Lupinus (Lupine)
Mertensia (Virginia Bluebells)
Phlox (Phlox)
Platycodon (Balloon Flower)
Primula (Primrose)
Pulmonaria (Lungwort)
Salvia (Sage)
Scabiosa (Pincushion Flower)
Stachys (Betony)
Stokesia (Stokes' Aster)
Tradescantia (Spiderwort)
Veronica (Speedwell)

Cool-Summer Lovers

These perennials are best when grown in climate zones that have cool summers, such as mountainous or coastal regions.

Aquilegia (Columbine)
Astilbe (False Spirea)
Delphinium (Delphinium)
Dicentra (Bleeding Heart)
Helleborus (Christmas Rose)
Ligularia (Groundsel)
Lupinus (Lupine)
Penstemon (Beardtongue)
Primula (Primrose)
Thalictrum (Meadowrue)

Hemerocallis (daylilies) offer attractive foliage, are excellent cut flowers, and come in a wide range of colors. They are particularly well suited to the climate of the South.

Best for the South

All of the following plants will perform well as far south as USDA zone 9. Those marked with an asterisk (*) are well adapted to zone 10.

*Acanthus (Bear's Breech)
Achillea (Yarrow)
Amsonia (Blue Star)
Anthemis (Golden Marguerite)
Armeria (Sea Pink)
Artemisia (Wormwood)
Aruncus (Goatsbeard)
Asclepias (Butterfly Flower)
Baptisia (False Indigo)
Bergenia (Bergenia)
Brunnera (Siberian Bugloss)
Campanula (Harebell)
Ceratostigma (Blue Plumbago)
*Chrysanthemum (Chrysanthemum)
Cimicifuga (Bugbane)
*Coreopsis (Calliopsis)
Dicentra (Bleeding Heart)
Digitalis (Foxglove)
Echinacea (Coneflower)
Echinops (Globe Thistle)
*Euphorbia (Spurge)
Filipendula (Queen of the Prairie)
Gaillardia (Blanket Flower)
Geum (Avens)
Grasses: All. *Cortaderia (Pampas Grass)
Helianthus (Sunflower)
Heliopsis (Heliopsis)
Helleborus lividus var. *corsicus* (Corsican Hellebore)
*Hemerocallis (Daylily)
Heuchera (Coral Bells)
*Hibiscus (Rose Mallow)
*Hosta (Plantain Lily)
Iris (Iris)

Kniphofia (Torch Lily)
*Liatris (Blazing Star)
Lychnis (Campion)
Lythrum (Loosestrife)
Mertensia (Virginia Bluebells)
Monarda (Bee Balm)
Penstemon (Beardtongue)
Phlox (Phlox)
Platycodon (Balloon Flower)
Rudbeckia (Black-eyed Susan)
Salvia (Sage)
Scabiosa (Pincushion Flower)
*Sedum (Stonecrop)
Solidago (Goldenrod)
Stachys (Betony)
*Stokesia (Stokes' Aster)
Tradescantia (Spiderwort)
Veronica (Speedwell)

Tolerant of Dry Soil

These perennials will tolerate drought and poor, dry soil better than most.

Achillea (Yarrow)
Amsonia (Blue Star)
Anthemis (Golden Marguerite)
Armeria (Sea Pink)
Artemisia (Wormwood)
Asclepias (Butterfly Flower)
Aurinia (Basket-of-Gold)
Baptisia (False Indigo)
Belamcanda (Leopard Flower)
Chrysanthemum parthenium (Feverfew)
Coreopsis (Calliopsis)
Dianthus (Pink)
Echinops (Globe Thistle)
Euphorbia (Spurge)
Gaillardia (Blanket Flower)

Geranium (Cranesbill)
Grasses: *Andropogon* (Little Bluestem)
     Cortaderia (Pampas Grass)
     Elymus (Blue Lyme Grass)
     Festuca (Blue Fescue)
     Miscanthus (Eulalia Grass)
Hemerocallis (Daylily)
Iris, Pacific Coast varieties (Pacific Coast Iris)
Kniphofia (Torch Lily)
Liatris scariosa (Tall Gayfeather)
Rudbeckia (Black-eyed Susan)
Salvia (Sage)
Sedum (Stonecrop)
Solidago (Goldenrod)
Stachys (Betony)
Thermopsis (False Lupine)
Tradescantia (Spiderwort)

Tolerant of Moist Soil

The following perennials are good choices for that difficult low, soggy spot in the garden.

Aruncus (Goatsbeard)
Astilbe (False Spirea)
Caltha (Marsh Marigold)
Cimicifuga (Bugbane)
Filipendula (Queen of the Prairie)
Hibiscus (Rose Mallow)
Iris kaempferi (Japanese Iris)
Iris pseudacorus (Yellow Flag)
Lobelia cardinalis (Cardinal Flower)
Lysimachia (Loosestrife)
Lythrum (Purple Loosestrife)
Mertensia (Virginia Bluebells)
Monarda (Bee Balm)
Primula japonica (Japanese Primrose)
Tradescantia (Spiderwort)
Trollius (Globe Flower)

For the Shade

Some of the following plants tolerate shade well, while others actually prefer it. For most shade lovers, the light, filtered shade of high tree limbs is ideal. Those marked with an asterisk (*) are tolerant of deeper shade. Remember that no plant will survive long in deep, black darkness.

Acanthus (Bear's Breech)
Alchemilla (Lady's Mantle)
Anemone (Anemone)
Aquilegia (Columbine)
Aruncus (Goatsbeard)
Astilbe (False Spirea)
Bergenia (Bergenia)
* *Brunnera* (Siberian Bugloss)
Campanula (Harebell)
Ceratostigma (Blue Plumbago)
Chrysogonum (Golden Star)
Cimicifuga (Bugbane)
Dicentra (Bleeding Heart)
Digitalis (Foxglove)
Doronicum (Leopard's Bane)
Euphorbia (Spurge)
Filipendula (Queen of the Prairie)
Helleborus (Christmas Rose)
Hemerocallis (Daylily)
Heuchera (Coral Bells)
* *Hosta* (Plantain Lily)
Iris sibirica (Siberian Iris)
Ligularia (Groundsel)
Lobelia cardinalis (Cardinal Flower)
Lysimachia (Loosestrife)
Mertensia (Virginia Bluebells)
Monarda (Bee Balm)
* *Polygonatum* (Solomon's Seal)

Primula (Primrose)
* *Pulmonaria* (Lungwort)
Thalictrum (Meadowrue)
Trollius (Globe Flower)

Cut Flowers

Not all of the perennials useful for cut flowers will be found in this list, only some of the best. The flowers of those plants marked with an asterisk (*) are especially suitable for drying and preserving.

Acanthus (Bear's Breech)
Achillea (Yarrow)
Anemone (Anemone)
Anthemis (Golden Marguerite)
Aster (Aster)
Chrysanthemum (Chrysanthemum)
Coreopsis (Calliopsis)
Delphinium (Delphinium)
Dianthus (Pink)
Digitalis (Foxglove)
Echinacea (Coneflower)
* *Echinops* (Globe Thistle)
Gaillardia (Blanket Flower)
Geum (Avens)
Grasses: All.
* *Gypsophila* (Baby's Breath)
Helenium (Sneezeweed)
Helianthus (Sunflower)
Heliopsis (Heliopsis)
Hemerocallis (Daylily)
Heuchera (Coral Bells)
Hosta (Plantain Lily)
Iris (Iris)
Kniphofia (Torch Lily)
Liatris (Blazing Star)
Lupinus (Lupine)
Paeonia (Peony)
Papaver (Poppy)
Rudbeckia (Black-eyed Susan)
Scabiosa (Pincushion Flower)
* *Solidago* (Goldenrod)
Stokesia (Stokes' Aster)
Veronica (Speedwell)

Attractive Foliage

The following plants are especially valuable for their foliage effect. The notation (C) signifies a coarse, bold texture; (M) a medium texture; and (F) a fine texture. The notation (G) indicates gray or silvery foliage, and (E) indicates that the plant is ever-

green. Many plants that generally are evergreen may be only semievergreen the farther north they are grown.

Acanthus (C) (Bear's Breech)
Alchemilla (M) (Lady's Mantle)
Amsonia (F) (Blue Star)
Armeria (F, E) (Sea Pink)
Artemisia (F, G) (Wormwood)
Aruncus (C) (False Spirea)
Aurinia (G) (Basket-of-Gold)
Baptisia (M) (False Indigo)
Bergenia (C, E) (Bergenia)
Coreopsis verticillata (F) (Threadleaf Coreopsis)
Dianthus (F) (Pink)
Euphorbia (M) (Spurge)
Grasses: All.
Helleborus (E) (Christmas Rose)
Hemerocallis (E, selected varieties) (Daylily)
Heuchera (E) (Coral Bells)
Hosta (C) (Plantain Lily)
Iris kaempferi (M) (Japanese Iris)
Iris sibirica (M) (Siberian Iris)
Kniphofia (M) (Torch Lily)
Ligularia (C) (Groundsel)
Paeonia (M) (Peony)
Polygonatum (M) (Solomon's Seal)
Pulmonaria (M) (Lungwort)
Salvia × *superba* (G) (Perennial Salvia)
Sedum (M) (Stonecrop)
Stachys byzantina (G) (Wooly Betony)
Thalictrum (F) (Meadowrue)

Fragrance

Some of the more fragrant perennials are included in the list below. An asterisk (*) indicates that the plant foliage is fragrant when crushed or bruised.

* *Achillea* (Yarrow)
* *Anthemis* (Golden Marguerite)
* *Artemisia* (Wormwood)
Cimicifuga (Bugbane)
Dianthus (Pink)
Dictamnus (Gas Plant)
Filipendula (Queen of the Prairie)
Hemerocallis (selected varieties) (Daylily)
Hosta plantaginea (Fragrant Plantain Lily)
Iris, bearded (Bearded Iris)
* *Monarda* (Bee Balm)
Paeonia (Peony)
Phlox paniculata (Garden Phlox)
Primula (selected varieties) (Primrose)
* *Salvia* (Sage)

FROM THE GROUND UP

If you give perennials the little extra care they need at planting time and during the fall and winter months, they will reward you with a spectacular spring and summer display, year after year.

Above: Towering spires of deep lavender delphiniums, white *Lilium testaceum*, and low-growing chartreuse *Alchemilla mollis* are combined in this garden at Sissinghurst Castle in England. Every gardener with a sound knowledge of basic perennial care can create similar successful combinations. Left: The effort required to create a scene like the one shown here may be far less than you think. Perennials are, for the most part, a group of sturdy plants that are very willing to grow. Shown here are: *Chrysanthemum parthenium*, *Astilbe* 'Fire', *Heliopsis* 'Greenheart', *Lilium regale*, *Cimicifuga racemosa*, and *Filipendula rubra*.

Perennials, like most plants, require only the basics for good growth: a reasonably fertile soil, good drainage, sufficient sun and water, and a little tender loving care. With a little attention to the basics in the beginning, most perennials will remain healthy for years.

In this section we'll give you the principles for providing these basics. We'll tell you step by step how to evaluate your soil and bring it into excellent condition for perennials. We'll also tell you where to find the plants you want and, for those interested in economy and a rewarding gardening venture, how to start your perennials from seed. We'll also cover transplanting, staking, fertilizing, watering, pest and disease control, and even tell you how to divide the plants—in short, just about everything you need to know to grow healthy, vigorous perennials.

Soil Preparation

Some areas of the country have naturally occurring "good soil" that requires little attention from the gardener. These soils have plenty of organic matter, ample nutrients, and a structure that allows good air and moisture circulation and a strong foothold for roots.

If this is your soil, count yourself blessed, because there's nothing quite like having quality soil to garden in without expending any effort. But if you're not so fortunate, don't gamble on trying to garden without improving your soil. Nothing is so disappointing as having to deal with a difficult soil that produces minimum success and a multitude of problems.

The best time to prepare your soil for perennials is at least a couple of months before you intend to plant. This waiting period allows any amendments you add to the soil to take effect. Most perennials are planted in fall or spring, so soil should be prepared in the summer for fall planting, or in the fall for spring planting.

The first quality to look at in your soil is its texture. The two extremes in texture are clay and sand. Clay consists of microscopic particles bound too closely together to allow much drainage or root penetration. Sand does not retain enough moisture and drains so quickly that nutrients are leached out. If your soil has too much sand or clay, it may also have a poor structure, meaning that it will not form the crumblike particles needed by most plants for good growth. Both clay and sand, however, have their virtues, and in the right combinations make excellent soils.

There is a simple test for texture and structure that gardeners have used for centuries. First take a shovel or cultivator and work up the soil a bit; then take a handful, squeeze it in your palm, open your hand, and see what happens. If the soil holds together for a few seconds and then crumbles apart, you have a good-quality soil known as a loam soil. If it just sits in your hand in one big lump, it either has too high a clay content or is too wet. If the weather has been fairly dry, you know that your soil has too much clay, and you'll want to improve it. If the soil doesn't adhere to itself but flows through your fingers, you know it's too sandy and will need some work. (Note that this test is also a good one to see if your soil is dry enough to cultivate or to plant.)

Improving Your Soil

Improving soils that are too clayey or sandy is an easy task: you merely add organic matter—and plenty of it—into the top layer. Organic matter is simply matter that was once living; and adding it is the best thing you can do for your soil. It holds water and nutrients like a sponge, increasing the soil's capacity for both; it opens and loosens the soil; and as it breaks down into *humus* (the dark, decayed substance that gives soil its characteristic color), it forms gluelike materials that stick soil particles together in little crumbs, forming a soft, rich medium perfect for good root growth. Such a loose soil of good structure and texture is called a *friable* soil.

Almost all organic materials are good for your soil, and there are many available. They include those you can find at most nurseries and garden centers, such as shredded bark, chunk bark, leaf mold, peat moss, and manures; and those that you produce yourself or get from other sources, such as sawdust, hay, lawn and garden clippings, weeds, corncobs, and compost.

How much organic matter to add depends upon the condition of your soil and the depth to which you want to condition it. If your garden has been growing healthy plants, or even a healthy weed crop, and if you've noticed no drainage problems such as water from rain or sprinklers puddling up, you may not need to add much. Generally, it's almost impossible to add too much organic matter, and any amount you do add will improve the soil quality. (Extremely soft, fluffy, acid soils that are mostly organic matter are an exception.) One widely observed rule of thumb is to add an amount equal to one-third to one-half the depth of soil you want to condition; for example, a 2- to 3-inch layer over 6 inches of soil, a 4- to 6-inch layer over 12 inches of soil, and so on.

If the organic matter is not completely decayed and does not already have added nitrogen (if it does, the label will say "nitrogen-fortified"), you'll need to add some. Two pounds of ammonium sulfate (or the equivalent) per 100 feet of space will prevent the organic matter from taking from the soil the nitrogen that decay bacteria need to break it down further.

With very sticky clay soils, another amendment of great value is gypsum. Gypsum often helps to improve the structure of clay soils. It should be added at a rate of about 5 pounds per 100 square feet of space. If it works, drainage will be improved almost immediately. Extremely heavy clay soils are another problem entirely, and in some rare cases cannot by any means be made into good soil. If you suspect that you have one of these soils, before you go to the expense of trying to improve it, contact your local nurseryman or County Extension Agent for more information.

Soil pH

At the same time you test the condition of your soil, it's a good idea to check its pH. Many states offer free or low-cost pH tests (for details call your County Extension Agent); or, you probably can find inexpensive testing kits at your local garden center. The test is easy to perform.

The letters *pH* stand for the chemical term *potential hydrogen*, which is a measure of acidity and alkalinity. The pH scale runs from 0, extremely acid, to 14, extremely alkaline, with the middle of the scale, 7, the neutral point. The vast majority of perennials grow best in neutral or slightly acid soils.

If your soil is extremely acid, you can add ground limestone to correct it. If alkalinity is a problem, you can correct it by adding a garden sulfur or ferrous sulfate. Both are avail-

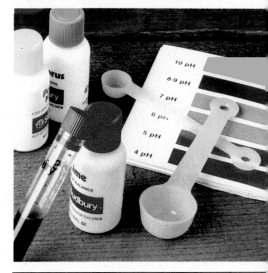

able at nurseries and garden centers. Ask your nursery manager or County Extension Agent for the specific rates to apply. Tell him or her the present pH of your soil, the type of soil you have, and what pH level you are trying to achieve.

Fertilizer

At the same time you add organic matter and lime or sulfur to the soil, it's good to add a complete fertilizer as well. Packaged dry fertilizers are the easiest to apply. Choose a formulation such as 5–10–5 (the numbers refer to the percentages of nitrogen, phosphorus, and potassium, in that order), one that is high in phosphorus and relatively low in nitrogen, and apply it at about 3 to 5 pounds per 100 square feet. A fertilizer high in nitrogen content may stimulate leafy growth at the expense of flowers. Phosphorus stimulates both root growth and the formation of flowers. Potassium, or potash, contributes to stem strength and increases resistance to disease.

Cultivating the Soil

If the simple hand test mentioned earlier indicated that your soil is ready to be worked, the first step is to clear the site of all weeds. It's far better to pull the weeds out by hand than to hoe or scrape them off. The next step is to turn the soil over, being careful to remove any remaining weed roots: the spade or rototiller will chop these up if you don't get them and in effect multiply the number of weeds you'll have to deal with later.

After the site is clear of weeds, spread the organic matter, fertilizer, and, if needed, the lime or sulfur, all in a more or less even layer on top.

There is no point in being stingy at this stage: small amounts of any amendment will not change the soil structure appreciably; so spread the organic matter around with a free hand. If you're using peat moss, be sure it is moist when you take it from the bag. If not, moisten it with warm water while it is still in the bag, or use a wetting agent especially made for this purpose, available at garden centers.

Now you are ready to work the soil. For some gardeners, this means using a shovel, spade, or digging fork to turn the top layer, breaking it into smaller pieces as they go. Those with fairly large gardens use a power tiller. One method is not necessarily better for the soil than the other, but if you are using a power tiller, keep these points in mind: first, don't overdo it; a couple of passes should make a good planting bed and any more may make the soil so fine that the first application of water will produce a thick crust on the soil surface. Second, most power tillers are limited in the depth they can cultivate, usually to 6 to 8 inches. It is generally believed that the deeper you cultivate the soil for perennials (and this is especially true with heavy clay soils), the better will be your results. If you want to produce the best possible planting bed, you will have to cultivate by hand. And you may want to use the method known as "double-digging."

Double Digging. Double-digging involves digging the top 10 or so inches of soil and moving it to a holding area. You then spade the subsoil layer, working organic matter into it as you go, to a depth of another 10 inches or so. Finally, you amend the topsoil

with organic matter and fertilizer and layer it on top of the improved subsoil.

The only practical way to double-dig a bed is to do it with a spade, as shown in the illustration. It is a laborious job that requires much effort and patience, and this is not everybody's cup of tea. Many knowledgeable gardeners point out that since most of the feeder roots of perennials are in the top layer of the soil, cultivating 6 to 8 inches deep is quite enough to produce healthy, vigorous plants. Still, double-digging produces an excellent planting bed that can remain untouched for years afterward.

Power Tillers. If you prefer to use a power tiller to incorporate the amendments into the soil, remember that the heavier the machine, the easier the work. Power tillers are available for rental in most communities.

Make sure the soil is sufficiently moist, but not wet, before you begin. If not, water the soil thoroughly, then wait a few days to let it dry out somewhat before you start tilling. If your soil is unusually heavy, it may take several passes with the tiller to cultivate the soil to a depth of 6 inches; but remember not to overcultivate the soil.

After cultivating, use a large metal rake to smooth the surface. After leaving the bed fallow for a couple of months, you'll be ready to plant. Be sure to keep weeds picked in the meantime to keep them at a minimum in the garden.

If you are interested in learning more about the nature of soil, how to change its quality, and about the role of fertilizers, be sure to see Ortho's *Fertilizers, Soils & Water*.

For small areas, the easiest way to cultivate the soil is by using a little muscle power and a shovel. For larger beds, you may want to use a power tiller (see text).

Double-digging is a time-honored but nonetheless laborious method of deep cultivation. The top layer of soil is first stripped off to a depth of 10 inches or so. An additional 10 inches of sublayer soil is then cultivated and amended with organic matter. The top layer of soil is then replaced after it, too, has been amended. Double-dug beds remain in excellent condition for many years.

Right: Most large nurseries and garden centers offer a good selection of perennials—some of which may already be in bloom—in 1-gallon cans. This way of starting a perennial garden is relatively expensive, but it allows the gardener to see exactly what a plant's foliage and flowers look like before planting. Far right: Perennials are available in many forms: as bare-root dormant plants from mail-order nurseries, in small plastic cell packs, in 4- and 6-inch pots, in 1-gallon cans, and, for those with patience, from the seed rack.

Plant Sources

The fact that perennials have been the favorite plants of generations of gardeners is good testimony to their value in any present-day garden. It is the legacy of these gardeners that today there are thousands of varieties of perennials to choose from, a selection to keep the most ambitious gardener content for a lifetime.

After you have decided what style of planting you want—bed, border, plants simply spotted through the landscape, or container plants—you will want to make up a plant list. You can compile the list from the Plant Selection Guide (starting on page 47) in this book, from other books, from garden catalogs, or from plants you have seen growing in other gardens or at a local nursery or garden center.

The best sources for plants are nurseries and garden catalogs, but don't fail to consider plants given by or exchanged with gardening friends. As perennials outgrow their alloted spaces, they need to be divided, and divisions from established plants are generally as good as those available from nurseries and catalogs. It's good to remember, though, that any plant that has outgrown a neighbor's garden probably will do the same in yours. Plants most frequently handed over the back fence are usually the most vigorous and invasive ones. It's best to think twice about where you plant them, and allow plenty of room for expanding growth.

Nurseries. If you're fortunate, you'll have a nursery close by that handles a good selection of perennials. These most often will be climati-cally adapted to your region. And a large nursery or garden center probably will offer perennials in several different stages of development.

More and more nurseries are offering perennials as first-year seedlings planted in flats or plastic containers called "cell packs" or "six packs." These may take another year of growth in the garden to produce a good display of flowers, but the price represents a considerable savings over those in 4-inch pots or gallon cans.

You'll see the greatest selection of potted perennials at your nursery during their season of bloom, the spring and summer months. Obviously it is much easier to sell plants as an "impulse item" when they are in full bloom; but this is also an aid to the novice gardener who doesn't mind spending the extra money to see exactly what he or she is getting.

When choosing nursery plants, try to select those that are bushy and compact; avoid any that are sparse and leggy. A healthy green leaf color is a good sign that the plants have been well cared for. It's tempting to pick out plants that are in full bloom, but plants without flowers are usually more satisfactory in the long run. Also, fresh stock is usually preferable to plants that have been growing in small containers for many months. It's a good idea to find out the days the nursery receives its shipment from the wholesale grower. If you're there when the truck is unloaded, not only will you get the freshest plants, but you'll also be able to pick from the widest selection.

Catalogs. If the selection of perennials is limited at your local nursery or garden centers, you'll need to rely on ordering from catalogs or starting your own perennials from seed. The list on page 27 contains many reputable sources for seeds and plants. Some of the catalogs feature perennials almost exclusively; others include other garden plants. If you are looking for hard-to-find varieties, the specialty catalogs are best.

If there is a charge for the catalog, it is usually nominal, and most companies refund its cost with your first order. Some companies print two catalogs: a spring selection and a fall selection. The spring catalog (the one most companies offer, and the one that most excites gardeners) is mailed in the winter; the fall catalog is usually sent out in the spring. This gives gardeners a chance to make their choices and have the plants shipped at the proper planting time.

Live perennials ordered from catalogs usually arrive one of two ways: as dormant, bare-root plants with roots enclosed in damp sphagnum moss, wrapped in plastic; or as potted plants with the top growth visible. Companies generally are careful to note where the order is being sent and will wait to ship until the weather there is suitable for planting.

Catalogs serve another important function for the gardener: to sit down with a catalog filled with enticing descriptions and colorful illustrations, especially when the garden outside is in a state of winter drabness, is pure pleasure and a great inspiration toward the new gardening season.

Top: The first step in starting perennials from seed is to fill a flat with a moistened planting medium and to plant seeds to the depth indicated on the seed packet. For straight rows of seedlings, make depressions in the planting medium, using the edge of a ruler. Middle: Lightly sprinkle the soil with water and slip the flat into a clear or black plastic bag, depending on whether or not the seeds need light or darkness for germination. Bottom: Once the seeds have germinated, remove the plastic and transplant the seedlings into individual containers.

Starting Your Own

Starting your perennials from seed is an intriguing and rewarding venture, if you have the patience and the room to try it. Planting seed has several advantages, not the least of which is that it is the least expensive way to procure a large number of plants. Another benefit is that you are not limited to the varieties offered at your local nursery, or to those available as plants from mail-order sources. Selections offered by nurseries that specialize in perennials often include rare varieties you may want to try.

Always buy the best-quality seeds you can find, and plant them the year you receive them: the freshest seeds give the best results. Some perennials are particular about the conditions they need in order to germinate. Read the instructions included with the seeds carefully and do your best to provide the conditions called for. The Plant Selection Guide, starting on page 47, includes instructions for those perennials it lists with unusual seed-starting requirements.

Over a period of time, gardeners develop their own favorite methods for starting seeds. The following is one way that works well for many perennials.

Getting Started. The equipment should include a number of seed flats or trays with drainage holes, a top-quality growing medium such as *milled* sphagnum moss (not the product commonly seen in plastic bags, but one with an exceedingly fine texture), heating cables to provide warm soil (if necessary), and some type of fluorescent light unit whose height above the flats can be adjusted.

First, moisten the milled sphagnum in a plastic bag or other container, place it in the flats, and firm it down slightly to form a smooth, even surface. You can scatter the seeds over the surface, or plant them in rows. Sow the seeds thinly, tapping them out of the packet slowly for an even spread.

The next steps depend upon the specific requirements of the seeds. Some need light and heat to germinate and others require darkness and fairly cool temperatures. Some have periods of dormancy that need to be overcome by chilling in the refrigerator. Some seeds, in order to germinate most quickly, need to be soaked or to have their seed coats filed. Be sure to check closely the instructions that come with the seeds.

Moisture is critical in seed germination, and it's best not to take chances. The best way to supply moisture is to water from the bottom, not the top. You can place the flat or tray in the sink or in a larger pan, such as a cookie sheet, pour water into the sink or pan, and allow it to seep up into the soil. To maintain humidity, it's best to place a sheet of clear plastic over seeds that need light to germinate, and a sheet of black plastic over those that need darkness. Be sure, however, to remove the plastic as soon as the seeds start to sprout; otherwise, you'll be risking fungus disease that can wipe out the seedlings.

Maintaining moisture is especially critical with very fine, dustlike seeds, which have a tendency to dry out quickly.

Transplanting Seedlings. Once the seeds have germinated and have produced their second set of true leaves, they are ready to be planted into their own containers. Small peat pots are best, as these can be planted directly into the garden. Fill them with good-quality packaged soil mix and wet it down before you start to transplant, and be careful not to let the seedlings dry out between the time you remove them from the flat and the time they are safely in the new containers. This is one of the most common causes for plant loss.

Transplanting requires patience and dexterity. A flat pointed stick such as an old plant label works well to separate the seedlings and to ease them into the new soil. Use a light touch when firming the new soil around the roots of seedlings; too much pressure will squeeze the air from the soil, making it an unhealthy medium for the tender plants.

Many perennials do not take well to transplanting. Seeds of these should be sown directly into peat containers.

Seedlings in containers should be kept in a protected environment such as a lath house or cool greenhouse for several weeks. After they are established they can be moved to a somewhat less protected environment; but they are still not ready for the full brunt of the elements. They will need more or less constant watering during warm summer months, and applications of an all-purpose complete fertilizer every 4 to 6 weeks throughout the growing season to get them on their way. Within a year's time you should have quite a collection of healthy, good-size perennials ready to go into the garden.

Perennial seeds of course can be sown directly into the garden, but with varying degrees of success and usually a very low percentage of germination. Following the previous instructions will greatly increase germination and allow you to control your supply of plants.

For more detailed information on starting seeds, see Ortho's *All About Annuals.*

To plant dormant plants, remove any plastic wrapping from the rootball and carefully shake loose the packing material.

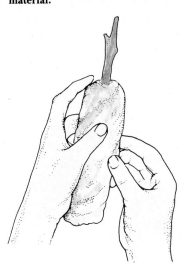

Inspect the roots. Remove any that are dry and brittle or that appear to have rotted.

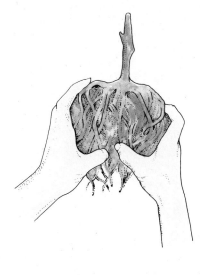

Without wasting any time, position the dormant plant in the hole so that the crown is at soil level. Backfill with soil and remove any air pockets, using gentle but firm pressure.

Transplanting Dormant Plants

If you ordered dormant plants from a catalog, they should arrive sometime in early spring. They won't look like much, but they are alive and should be treated with care. If the weather does not permit planting immediately, keep them in a cool, dark spot and make sure the sphagnum moss surrounding them doesn't dry out.

When the time comes to plant them in the garden, remove them from their plastic coverings, shake the moss off carefully, and inspect the roots. Remove any that are dry and brittle or appear to have rotted. Take as little time as possible before getting them into the ground: it doesn't take long for wind and sun to dry out the tiny roots that are essential to life during the critical first few weeks after transplanting.

Before planting, take a good look at your plan to make sure you know what plants you want in which locations and how far apart they should be spaced. Some gardeners place tiny stakes to indicate locations.

Dig the holes large enough so that roots won't be cramped when you spread them out. The depth of the hole will be determined by the root system of the plant. Generally speaking, the point where the roots meet the stem or crown should be placed right at or slightly below ground level.

After you have inserted the plant, pack the soil around the root system gently. When the hole is filled you can firm it down with your feet to make sure there are no empty spaces between roots and soil. Water the plant thoroughly. This is also the best time to label the plants for future reference.

If plants are grown in metal cans, have the cans cut to make removal easier. The rootball should be moist to avoid shattering.

After freeing any tangled or circled roots, position the plant in the hole slightly deeper than it was in the can. Backfill with reserved soil, remove any air pockets, and water immediately.

Transplanting Started Plants

If you ordered started plants from a mail-order source or purchased them in six packs or gallon cans from your garden center or nursery, the planting procedure is basically the same.

Small plants in six packs can be removed easily by pushing up on the bottom of the individual cell. Don't try to pull the plant out by the stem: it may not have an extensive root system and the top could break away from the roots. With a trowel, dig small holes roughly the same depth as the rootball. Take the plants out one by one and plant them *slightly* deeper than they were in the pack. Firm the soil around them and water thoroughly.

Larger perennials may be planted in plastic or tapered metal cans. Plants can be removed easily if the rootball is moist by turning the can over with your hand across the top and shaking it slightly. If the plants are in straight-sided metal cans and you plan on planting them right away, have the cans cut at the nursery. If you intend to hold the plants awhile before planting, leave the cans intact and cut them later yourself with a pair of tin snips. (Cut cans are almost impossible to water thoroughly.)

Be sure to loosen the circling roots around the rootball and spread them out before planting, so they won't girdle the plant. It's a good idea to rub the rootball with a fork or your hands to make sure the roots spread out into the soil.

Right: One time-honored way to support a clump of tall-growing perennials is to stick last year's twiggy prunings into the ground, all around the clump. As the plants grow, the plants can lean on the twigs and will eventually completely camouflage them. Below: Many gardeners like the convenience of liquid fertilizers for use as foliar feeds (see text) or for regular soil applications. Here, a special metering device draws the fertilizer solution from the bucket and mixes it with the water as it passes through the hose.

Staking

Staking is controversial among ardent perennial gardeners: some dislike the task so much that they refuse to plant any varieties that need it. There are two types of plants that require staking: those with tall single stalks, such as delphinium, hollyhocks, and gladiolus; and those with many floppy stems, such as asters, chrysanthemums, coreopsis, heliopsis, and carnations.

Tall, thin poles, such as the commonly available bamboo stakes, make the best supports for the single-stem plants. Simply place the stake an inch or so from the main stalk and shove it far enough into the ground to be stable. Attach the stalk to the stake with a plant tie, forming the tie into a figure eight, being careful not to cut into the stem but still allowing some natural back-and-forth movement.

The favored method for staking lower, bushier plants is to use the twining prunings from fruit or ornamental trees, cut into lengths of about 16 to 20 inches. When the plants are about half that height, push the dried branches into the ground, placing several in a circular pattern around the clump. These provide a natural framework to support the plant and will become less noticeable as the plant grows.

Fertilizing

Although not absolutely necessary, a midsummer feeding will benefit most plants. You can use the same product you used in conditioning your soil (preferably a dry fertilizer with a 5–10–5 or similar formulation), but apply it at a lower rate, about 2 pounds per 100 square feet. This will ensure that the plants are well fed and go into the winter as vigorous and healthy as possible.

If any individual plants in the garden seem to lag and need additional feeding during the growing season, you can mix a liquid flower fertilizer with water and apply it to those plants only. Most of the liquid formulations are fast-acting and it's easy to control the amount you apply, just the thing for "touch-up" feedings. It's best to make such feedings with half-strength or even weaker solutions: too little can be remedied; too much can't.

Liquid fertilizers are also valuable for *foliar feeding*, spraying the fertilizer mixture onto the leaves and stems of the plant. For perennials, early spring growth is usually limited by cold soil, even when the air is warm. Under such conditions soil microorganisms are not active to convert nutrients into forms the roots can absorb. But if the nutrients were available, the plant would grow. A nutrient spray to the foliage will provide immediate nourishment, allowing the plant to begin growth before the roots are able to absorb food from the soil.

Remember, though, that foliar feeding is a supplement to soil nutrition, not a substitute. Nutrients applied to foliage are absorbed and used by the plant quite rapidly; absorption begins within minutes after application, and with most nutrients is completed within one to two days.

Watering
The amount of water needed in the garden depends upon climate. Where summer rains are frequent you may need to irrigate only during an occasional dry spell; but in parts of the arid West and Southwest, watering is one of the gardener's biggest chores.

Whatever your climate, the simple rule for watering correctly is this: when you water, water well, and learn how long it takes the soil to dry out between waterings. The best way to tell if you've watered thoroughly is to take a trowel or shovel and check to see if the soil is moist 3 or 4 inches down. If it is, you know the water is reaching the root zone of the plants. This is absolutely necessary; superficial waterings are not only a waste, but they can actually harm plants by encouraging roots to grow toward the surface.

Watering a flower border or bed is best done with a canvas or plastic soaker hose laid more or less permanently among the plants. When you irrigate, turn the water on at a low level to keep the foliage as dry as possible. Try to water during the morning so that the garden can dry off a bit before nightfall: wet foliage will make the plants more susceptible to disease organisms. Of course, it is all right to spray plants occasionally with the hose or to use overhead

sprinklers to remove dust and sediment from the air, if you're careful to do it early enough that plants can dry before evening.

Mulching
When spring is definitely in the air, the perennials are in the ground, the soil has warmed, and you have pulled any weeds that have appeared, apply 2 to 3 inches of mulch over the bed or border, tapering it off gradually as you get close to the plants. (A thick layer of moist mulch right next to a plant's stem can encourage pests and disease.)

Applying mulch in spring keeps the soil temperature cooler, which helps root growth; keeps the soil moisture at a more even level, thus reducing the amount of water needed; keeps a

Look carefully at the rock wall and you'll see a hose permanently attached to the side. Soaker hoses are one of the best ways to water flower borders. They can be laid directly on the soil between plants.

Any gardener who has gardened for more than a year or two will probably be able to tell you about the benefits of a spring-applied organic mulch. From the standpoint of easing your weeding and watering chores, mulching is almost essential.

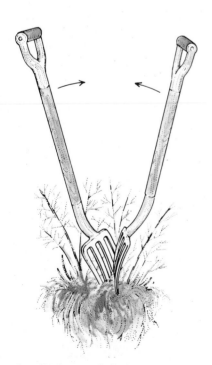

After digging up an overgrown perennial clump, you may find it necessary to use two spading forks, back-to-back, to divide the plant. Plant the new, smaller plants as you would a dormant plant.

majority of summer weeds from establishing themselves; and aids in the long-term development of a good soil structure. These virtues add up to better growing conditions for the plants and a much easier job of maintenance for you.

Almost any organic material can serve as mulch, and the most highly recommended are: finely ground fir or pine bark, pine needles, compost, well-rotted manure, and, where available, redwood soil conditioner. Peat moss unfortunately makes a poor mulch because it forms a crust on top that is nearly impenetrable by water.

If you have a large quantity of leaves each fall and access to a shredder, you can make an excellent mulch and soil amendment. Just shred the leaves, stack the product in piles, and leave it uncovered over the winter. By spring it will have decomposed. When the weather warms, turn the pile to let it dry out enough to apply easily.

In areas with extremely cold winters and a heavy snow cover, you'll want to protect your plants from the threat of *heaving*, the forcing out of the ground the plants can suffer as a result of alternate freezing and thawing. When the soil is thoroughly frozen to a depth of 2 inches, apply a layer of open, fluffy material such as pine boughs, excelsior, salt hay, or straw over the entire bed or border. This will keep the ground frozen until spring. Note that if you apply this protection any earlier, it may serve as a winter home for mice and other

rodents still afoot, who may then feed on the roots and crowns of your plants through the season.

Dividing

There are basically three reasons for dividing perennials: control of size, rejuvenation, and propagation.

The nature of most perennials is to grow larger every year, usually by spreading and making a larger clump. Left alone, the most vigorous growers can expand until they choke out many desirable plants. As the clumps expand, they begin to compete with themselves; those plants on the outer edge thrive in fresh soil, but those in the center suffer from competing for moisture, nutrients, light, and air. You can end up with a healthy circle of plants around a dying center, not an attractive sight.

Except in areas of the country with extremely cold winters (temperatures of -10° to -20° F), fall is the best time to divide perennials. The general rule is to divide spring- and summer-blooming perennials in late summer or fall, and to divide fall-blooming perennials in early spring, to give them a whole growing season to reestablish themselves. If you live in a climate with extreme winters, it's best to divide in early spring rather than subject newly planted divisions to the rigors of the weather.

Before the divide, decide what plants you want to save, which you want to dig out altogether, and which you want to replant elsewhere. To make digging and dividing easier, water the bed well a few days beforehand. So that you can see what you are doing, first prune the perennials severely, to 6 inches from the ground.

The actual dividing process is simple. Dig the entire clump out as completely as possible. If the center of the clump has died out, divide the living portion into smaller clumps to replant where you like. Where roots are so ensnarled that you can't simply pull the plants apart, you can cut them apart, but this is likely to do severe root damage. The best way to divide a stubborn clump is to insert two spading forks into it back-to-back, then press the handles toward each other, using the leverage at the tines to pry the clump apart.

The hole from which the clump was taken should be enriched with some organic matter and a handful of 0–10–10 fertilizer (or some similar formulation with no nitrogen). You can replace one or more of the divisions in the hole and replant the rest elsewhere or give them away to gardening friends.

Pest and Disease Control

As a group, perennials are remarkably free of most pest and disease problems. With a daily stroll in the garden, you can hold potential problems to a minimum just by keeping your eyes open for anything irregular: a chewed leaf, a disfigured bud, stunted foliage, a small patch of mildew or rust on a leaf, and so on.

If you take action at the first sign of attack, less damage is likely, and you'll also minimize the need for chemical controls.

You can avoid problems by taking these steps:

Keep old leaves picked up; they often harbor disease organisms and are safe hiding places for snails, slugs, and many damaging insects.

Pull weeds early, before they can compete with surrounding plants and produce seeds for more weeds. The best time to weed is when the ground is soft from rain or watering.

Remove and destroy any diseased leaves, flowers, or fruits. Do not put them on the compost pile. Disease spores can live from one season to the next.

Practice a thorough cleanup before winter sets in. Remove any debris and other likely homes for overwintering insects and diseases.

If a pest or disease does become a problem in your garden, consult the chart on this page for the best controls. The more common problems are listed in the chart. More specific pests and diseases are discussed for individual plants in the Plant Selection Guide beginning on page 47.

Aphids. Soft-bodied, green, brown, or reddish insects that suck plant juices. *Symptoms:* clusters of insects on shoots, flower buds or underside of leaves. Foliage and blooms stunted or deformed. Sticky honeydew attracts ants. *Solutions:* Lady beetles feed on aphids. Wipe out infestations with contact sprays such as Diazinon, Malathion, Sevin, or ORTHENE.

Beetles. Beetle larvae eat plant roots. *Symptoms:* Foliage, flowers, and stems are chewed, devoured, or have holes drilled in them. *Solutions:* Pick off beetles by hand or knock them into a can of kerosene and water. Spray with Diazinon, Malathion, or Sevin.

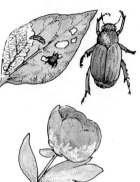

Botrytis Blight. (Gray Mold) A fungus disease that overwinters on infected plant parts. It attacks weak and dying foliage, flowers, and especially old, dying flowers. *Symptoms:* Grayish-brown growth on buds and flowers often appears fuzzy. The diseased flowers come apart easily when touched. *Solutions:* Pick off and destroy faded and infected blooms. Spray with fungicides. Read labels for recommendations.

Caterpillars. Larvae of moths and butterflies that feed on foliage, buds, and flowers. *Symptoms:* flower buds eaten or leaves rolled and tied around the pest and eaten from inside. Most often a problem in spring. *Solutions:* Cut out infested buds and leaves. Apply Diazinon or Sevin.

Damping Off. A fungus disease that is most often a problem in damp soil. *Symptoms:* Stems of young seedlings rot at ground level and fall over. Seedlings may also fail to emerge (preemergent damping off). *Solutions:* Do not overwater seedlings. Treat seeds with Captan, Phygon, Spergon, or Thiram.

Fungus Diseases. (Including powdery mildew and rust). Spread by wind and splashing water and overwinter on plant debris. *Symptoms:* Powdery mildew is shown by white powdery masses of spores on leaves, shoots, and buds; distorted shoots; or stunted foliage. Rust is shown by yellow dots and light green mottling on upper leaf surface opposite pustules of powdery, rust-colored spores on the lower surface. *Solutions:* For powdery mildew, apply Dinocap or PHALTAN. For rust, apply fungicides as recommended on labels. For both, remove and destroy all infected plant parts and debris.

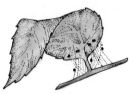

Mites. Minute pests that suck juices from underside of foliage. *Symptoms:* Stippled leaves appear dry; turn brown, red, yellow, or gray; then curl and drop off. Webs may be visible on the underside of leaves. *Solutions:* Clean up trash and weeds in early spring to destroy breeding places. Spray with Kelthane.

Thrips. Tiny, brownish-yellow, winged insects. *Symptoms:* flecked or silver-white streaking and stippling on foliage and flowers. *Solutions:* Cut off and dispose of spent blooms. Apply Diazinon, Malathion, ORTHENE, or Sevin.

Virus Diseases. (Including Mosaic and Aster Yellows) Spread by propagation of infected plants, aphids, and sometimes leafhoppers. *Symptoms:* mottling or mosaic patterns on leaves; stunted or distorted growth. *Solutions:* Dispose of entire affected plants. Prevention is the best control.

White Flies. Nymphs are scalelike, flat, oval, pale green, brown, or black, depending on the species. *Symptoms:* Pure white adults are easy to see. Leaves become mottled, may turn yellow and die. *Solutions:* Spray with Diazinon, Malathion, or ORTHENE.

THE ART OF PERENNIAL GARDENING

Throughout history, gardening with perennial flowers has caught the fancy of many gifted gardeners. On these pages, you will see some extraordinary gardens and learn some of the secrets of their success.

Above: A small garden at Sissinghurst in England. Complementing the earth tones of the brick cottage are: the bronze-foliage *Dahlia* 'East Court', yellow *Rudbeckia fulgida*, and the background planting of *Venidium arctotis* 'Flame'. Left: A very old perennial garden in England shows the work of a talented gardener. The combination of foliage textures, flower forms, and a subtle range of colors causes the viewer to look twice and walk away with new ideas and inspiration.

There is a unique dimension to gardening with perennials that for many gardeners greatly increases the pleasure of growing them: they are plants with a rich heritage, one that dates back through recorded history, and which attained rare heights in 19th-century England, when perennial gardening was given new life and refined into an art.

For many generations of English gardeners, perennials have been the backbone of the typical home garden. There had been no particular style or design associated with these gardens, just a love on the part of the gardener for the easily grown plants and their beautiful flowers. Later, these gardens would be termed "cottage gardens" (see page 10).

The familiarity and ease of culture of perennials led to some contempt for them during the Victorian era, when the demand for exotic plants rose to a peak. During this period, perennials were relegated to the backstage, considered by many as coarse "country cousins" to the more fashionable annuals that had been introduced to England and America from faraway lands.

True to typical Victorian fashion, it became the popular form of gardening among the wealthy to surround one's mansion with lavish displays of tender annuals planted in severely geometric patterns. Huge formal beds were imposed upon the landscape almost like artist's canvases, and made ready for temporary displays of color. Without regard for the individuality of the plants, the annuals were mass-planted in elaborate configurations designed primarily to be seen from an elevated viewing position. Today, you can see similar displays in public parks and municipal gardens, where annuals are frequently used in large beds to spell out words or to create specific designs. (It is also interesting to note that the term "bedding plants" originally referred only to annuals.)

Because these plants were gathered from countries with warm climates, they had to be coaxed into bloom in England in coal-heated greenhouses. It wasn't unusual for one display to be planted out, soon to be replaced with an entirely new one lest the owner and guests become bored by the same display. Obviously, this type of gardening demanded a great deal of time and money and a large staff of gardeners. As novel and exotic as the new plants were, their cultural requirements, as well as the prevailing style of planting them, put them beyond the reach of most gardeners.

The Return of Perennials

England has long been a nation of ardent gardeners, and it seems that each generation has had its own gardening "voice." In the late 19th century that voice belonged to William Robinson (1838–1935). Robinson not only pointed out the wastefulness of composing formal gardens of tender annuals, but labeled these gardens unnatural and unattractive as well. His was an attitude whose time had come.

Robinson favored "wild" or "natural" gardens, where special qualities of each plant could be highlighted. He was adamantly against using plants to further the geometry or architectural features of a garden. Robinson regularly put forth these somewhat strident views in his popular gardening magazine, *The Garden*.

In 1875 Robinson met Gertrude Jekyll (1843–1932), and because they shared similar viewpoints on gardening, Jekyll started contributing to the magazine.

Gertrude Jekyll began her career as an artist, but when her eyesight began to fail, she turned her artistic vision to gardening and writing about gardening. Although a woman of means, she was more influenced by the small, jumbled cottage gardens she observed in the countryside than by the great formal estate gardens. Scholars agree that it was Robinson who planted the seed of discontent regarding formal gardens, but it was Jekyll who brought the seed to flower in a popular form of gardening known as the "perennial border."

The cottage gardens that Jekyll admired must have impressed her as both a gardener and an artist. Although there was nothing grand about their scale or sophistication, these small gardens had a quality that the most monumental Victorian gardens lacked; namely, a respect for the plants themselves and a randomness in the way they were planted, a ran-

domness more commonly associated with gardens in the wild.

The rekindling of interest in perennial gardens would have stopped there if Jekyll had not been an artist. She took what she liked best about the cottage gardens, saw how they could be improved and made more beautiful, and refined her ideas. As a painter, she had an intuitive respect for color. To her, the perennial border represented the opportunity to plant beautiful, living paintings.

A young English architect named Edwin Lutyens (1869–1944) met Jekyll early in his career, and the two formed a long-lasting and important partnership.

Lutyens designed houses that were also a reaction against the formality and artifice of the Victorian period. Often built of native materials (stone, shingles, thatch, and the like), they had, regardless of their size, the cozy appearance of a cottage or farmhouse. He was a master at using stone, particularly for walls, paths, and garden pools. This stonework provided a strong architectural framework for the garden, but when com-

This American garden shows the distinct influence of the Jekyll–Lutyens traditions. The combination of rustic architecture and a casual cottage-style garden has a timeless appeal.

**"The first purpose of a garden is to give happiness and repose of mind, which is more often enjoyed in the contemplation of the homely border . . . , than in any of those great gardens where the flowers lose their identity, and with it their hold of the human heart, and have to take a lower rank as mere masses of color filling so many square yards of space."
—Gertrude Jekyll**

bined with Jekyll's sensitive and seemingly random plantings, the effect was anything but formal.

The partnership of Lutyens and Jekyll was a popular one, both in England and on the continent. Together they were commissioned to do many houses and gardens, some still in existence, and their continuing influence testifies to their skill and artistry.

The gardens Jekyll designed and wrote about were composed of plants chosen for their individual foliage and flower qualities, with a sharp eye for how each related to the scene as a whole. Although many of Jekyll's gardens were large, they were always planned on the human scale. They were filled primarily with perennials, but annuals, bulbs, shrubs, vines, and herbs also had their places.

Gardeners today may think of the classic perennial border as a rather formal style of gardening, but in England in the 19th and early 20th centuries, the popularization of perennials was a welcome relief from the formality and rigidity of gardening with annuals. The movement away from tender annuals was significant in two ways: it shifted the plants from freestanding beds or islands to the more practical garden border; and it was composed of plants climatically adapted to the region. The hardy perennial border was something any gardener, regardless of wealth or gardening space, could achieve and have success with.

Two famous gardens, still very much alive and flourishing, embody the spirit of Jekyll's teachings. One is Vita Sackville-West's garden at Sissinghurst Castle in Kent, England; the other the garden surrounding the home of the impressionist painter Claude Monet in Giverny, France. Both gardens are open to the public today.

Sissinghurst

Vita Sackville-West (1892–1962) and her husband, Sir Harold Nicolson, bought Sissinghurst Castle in 1930. Together they planned the gardens there, but it is her contribution that is best remembered because in addition to being a fine gardener, she was also a prolific writer. From 1947 to 1961 she wrote a popular weekly garden column for the *Observer*. These columns were gathered together at various times and published in book form. Several of these books are still available.

In the foreword of one collection titled *V. Sackville-West's Garden Book*, Phillipa Nicolson states that over the years Sackville-West never stopped experimenting, but gradually developed several ironclad principles of gardening:

"The first principle was ruthlessness. You must never retain for a second year what displeased you in the first. It must be eradicated. Secondly, she was the opponent of too much tidiness. Let self-seeded plants grow where they naturally fell; let wild flowers sometimes be allowed to invade the garden; if roses stray over

"Gardening is largely a question of mixing one sort of plant with another sort of plant, and of seeing how they marry happily together; and if you see that they don't marry happily, then you must hoick one of them. . . . That is the only way to garden."
—Vita Sackville-West

Vita Sackville-West's all-white garden at Sissinghurst continues to bloom today much as it did when she was alive. It is a fabulous garden that cannot help but make an impression on the visitor. Among the plants found in it are hydrangea, foxglove, candytuft, foamflower, lamb's ears, silver mound, delphiniums, and several old varieties of roses.

a path, the visitor must duck. But thirdly, there must be a plan—an architectural plan and a colour plan and a seasonal plan."

One of the most memorable and impressive of the individual gardens at Sissinghurst is the all-white garden. This garden has been the inspiration for many other similar gardens in all parts of the world. The principles on which it is based originated with Gertrude Jekyll's idea of a "tonal" garden, and when it was in its planning stages, Sackville-West wrote:

"For my own part, I am trying to make a grey, green, and white garden. This is an experiment which I ardently hope may be successful, though I doubt it.

"My grey, green, and white garden will have the advantage of a high yew hedge behind it, a wall along one side, a strip of box edging along another side, and a path of old brick along the fourth side. It is, in fact, nothing more than a fairly large bed, which has now been divided into halves by a short path of grey flagstones terminating in a rough wood seat. When you sit on this seat, you will be turning your back to the yew hedge, and from there I hope you will survey a low sea of grey clumps of foliage, pierced here and there with tall white flowers. I visualize the white trumpets of dozens of Regale lilies, grown three years ago from seed, coming up through the grey of southernwood and artemisia and cottonlavender, with grey-and-white edging plants such as *Dianthus* 'Mrs. Sinkins' and the silvery mats of *Stachys lanata*, more familiar and so much nicer under its English names of Rabbits' Ears or Saviour's Flannel. There will be white pansies, white peonies, and white irises with their grey leaves. . . at least, I hope there will be all of these things. I don't want to boast in advance about my grey, green, and white garden. It may be a ter-

rible failure. I wanted only to suggest that such experiments are worth trying, and that you can adapt them to your own taste and your own opportunities."

Her fears were unfounded. The white garden at Sissinghurst continues to bloom today, and each year visitors see the benefit of good planning.

Monet's *Le Pressoir*
Claude Monet (1840–1926) is unquestionably one of the greatest and bestloved French impressionist painters. In 1883 he moved himself, his future wife, and their collective family of eight children to a rented house in Giverny (about 40 miles northwest of Paris) known as *Le Pressoir* (the cider press). Monet immediately started a garden "so that there would be flowers to paint on rainy days." But it wasn't until nine years later, after he had purchased the house, that he began creating the garden which was to be immortalized in his paintings.

For the first few years, Monet and his crew of children planned and tended to the garden. By 1892 the garden had become so large that he hired a staff of six gardeners and built several greenhouses in which to start flowers. From Claire Joyes's excellent book, *Monet at Giverny*, comes this account of his gardening activity:

"Monet gave daily orders, inspecting the garden several times a day. No detail escaped him; he would correct a vista, recompose a clump of flowers, alter a pattern, and he insisted on the removal of fading blossoms. He planned his flower beds according to the principles that governed his palette, with light colours predominating and monochrome masses in juxtaposition. Very little soil was left bare in the garden; no flowers of a fancy variety, no coloured or variegated foliage were allowed, and he was particularly fond of briar roses and of star-

shaped dahlias with tubular petals.

"Although the layout of the flowerbed had a geometric basis, there was none of the formality of the typical French garden. Rectangles and straight lines disappeared under the spreading mats of nasturtium, wild geranium, aubretia and pink saxifrage. It was a painter's garden, where everything followed a certain rhythm, the supple tall stems of iris, lilies, foxgloves alternating with wild plumes of grasses and the bold masses of poppies and eschscholzias; where harmonies of tawny yellow, crimson and gold, saffron and blue were contrasted. Every item in the garden was designed to play a part; even the straight furrows in the raked garden paths were not a chance effect."

Monet died in 1926, leaving the house and garden to his son, Michel Monet. The son did not care in any special way for Giverny, and for over fifty years the estate was abandoned, during which time both the house and the garden fell into complete disrepair.

In 1966 Michel Monet died and willed the property to the *Institut de France*. After the *Institut* named Ger-

Monet's garden at Giverny, France, as it looks today, 2 years after the restoration was completed. The painting on the opposite page depicts this same scene.

ald Van der Kamp as the Conservator of the Claude Monet Foundation at Giverny, he faced the familiar and difficult task of finding the funds for the restoration process. The task was helped considerably by an early contribution of over one million dollars from an American benefactress, Lila Acheson Wallace.

After several years of painstaking work, the house and garden at Giverny were opened to the public for the first time in the summer of 1980. Today the gardens bloom again, and the house looks as it did when Monet lived there. From all accounts, a visit to Giverny is one well worth making.

Garden Restoration

For one reason or another, more and more people are buying older homes, with the intention of authentically restoring them in the way that corresponds to their particular period in architectural history. Large and small Victorian homes, rustic Craftsman bungalows, colonial farmhouses, and brownstone rowhouses frequently receive massive investments of effort and energy from new owners. Once the restoration work is completed, though, the gardens often need the same care and eye for detail that went into work on the house, in order to complete the picture. In almost all cases, unique period architecture had an equally unique style of gardening associated with it.

If you are interested in restoring a garden to fit a period house, you may be frustrated in trying to locate information on what the garden might have looked like in the past, and what types of plants might have been grown there. Local libraries, historical societies, and title companies often maintain large collections of photographs taken in much earlier times. You may not find a picture of your own house as it looked way back when, but you will begin to get a feel-

ing for what the gardens were like during the period by carefully scrutinizing these old photographs. And don't overlook the opportunity to talk with elderly neighbors; they may have vivid recollections of what the surrounding gardens once looked like.

Although there are few books available today that deal solely with period gardens, there are many books that deal with specific architectural styles. Many of these offer chapters relating to gardens and appropriate landscape styles. Even if no landscape information is given, photographs in architecture books can often give you ideas for creating a garden that is in keeping with the style of your house.

A restored Colonial garden at Williamsburg, Virginia, shows how the creation of an appropriate garden can complete the "period" picture.

PLANT SELECTION GUIDE

Use this guide to help you plan and design your garden or to determine the needs of perennials you already have. From the over one hundred perennials listed, you will be able to select plants for specific effects or to solve problems.

Above: An upright effect is created by this combination of *Iris sibirica, Thalictrum aquilegifolium, Lychnis chalcedonica, Papaver orientalis,* and *Dictamnus albus.* Left: This complimentary color scheme is achieved by combining the perennial yellow *Aurinia saxatilia* and the blue-purple bulb *Scilla* (bluebells). A few peonies have been added for interest and variety of form.

Including an enormous number of cultivars and varieties, there are literally thousands of perennials from which to choose. How, then, do you pick the best ones for your garden?

We have begun the selection process here. While this guide by no means presents all of the available perennials, we have chosen species and varieties that are the most dependable, the most widely available, and the most adaptable to a wide range of climate and cultural conditions. We have also included some others that fit special conditions or special uses in the garden or landscape.

In choosing perennials for your own garden, you may find it best to first skim through the guide, noting the plants that catch your eye and jotting them down on a piece of paper. If you are looking for plants to meet specific needs, the lists on page 24–27 will help you locate them. The

chart on page 18 will show you when they flower and what combinations and sequences of bloom are possible.

The next step is to read about the plants in more detail, keeping in mind these three questions.

Will this plant work? This is a question of function, whether the plant fills the intended role. Color, size, shape, texture, and bloom date should all be considered.

Will it grow in my garden? Many complex and varying factors enter into this question; but if the plant is hardy in your region, and if the requirements of soil, moisture, and light that we describe fit your conditions, then the chances of success are excellent.

Will this plant please me? This question addresses the personal tastes of the gardener. While seemingly an obvious one, it is surprising how often this all-important criterion is overlooked in the rush of sorting through the maze of cultural instructions and and opinions of others. It does little good to choose a plant because it fits and thrives in your garden, when you do not like it.

To give you as complete a picture as possible of each plant, we have included detailed information on physical characteristics and cultural requirements. Some of this information is of necessity generalized, and may need to be adjusted for your area. For example, bloom dates and the best times for planting and dividing do vary regionally. In this guide these times apply to USDA Climate Zone 6, which, as you can see on the map on this page, extends roughly on a line from Boston through Kansas City and into the Southwest. This "median" climate will serve as a general guide to give you some idea when to expect flowers, and when to plant and divide.

Bloom dates not only vary sometimes among climate zones, but can even vary from year to year in the same garden, by days or even weeks, according to such factors as weather and horticultural practices. Planting and dividing in fall may be recommended for some areas, and in spring for the same plant in a different area.

No one book can possibly tell you how plants perform in all of the diverse climatic conditions throughout the country; and for this reason we strongly suggest that you double-check how the choices you make from this plant guide will perform in your specific area and climate. You can find this information from such sources as nurseries, agricultural extension agents, universities, botanic gardens, garden clubs, and gardening neighbors.

Beyond serving as a handy reference and a means of introducing and familiarizing yourself with the perennials, we hope this guide will serve as inspiration and as a springboard for your own further explorations into the vast and intriguing world of perennial gardening.

Acanthus mollis 'Latifolius'

Acanthus mollis
(Bear's Breech)
Acanthus family. Native to the Mediterranean region.

Bear's breech is grown for its clumps of immense, coarse, glossy leaves and tall flower spikes. It is usually considered more a landscape plant than a border perennial.

The dark green, deeply lobed leaves grow to 2 feet long, in basal clusters often 2 feet high and 4 feet wide. The foliage is imposing and effective from March to October.

The flowers are creamy white, lavender, or rose, with greenish or purplish bracts, and appear along upright stems 2 to 3 feet tall. They bloom in late spring and early summer.

How to start: Best planted from divisions or nursery plants in spring.

Where to plant: Best in moist, rich loam with good drainage, but it performs reasonably well in dry sandy soil. It prefers filtered shade but tolerates full sun in cool climates. It tolerates drought, but foliage will be more lush with adequate moisture. In the northern limits of its range, plant in a warm, protected location, and mulch over winter. Space plants 3 to 4 feet apart. Bear's breech is a tender perennial, hardy in zones 8 through 10.

Care: Easy. Remove spent flower stalks. To grow for foliage alone, remove stalks as they appear. The roots spread a considerable distance underground and the plant forms spreading clumps, like bamboo; so confine the roots unless you want a large stand. Snails and slugs can be a problem. The plant rarely requires division for rejuvenation, but is easily propagated by that method. Divide any time from October to March.

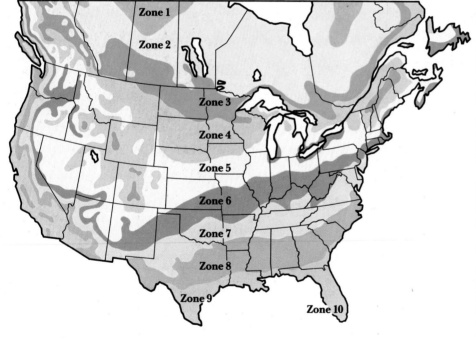

Climate Zones of the United States
Use this zone map to find your climate zone. Remember that these zones are approximate, based on average data, and that your local climate can be warmer or colder, especially in mountain regions. This map is based on the USDA map of climate zones.

Approximate range of average annual minimum temperature for each zone.

Zone 1	Below	−50°F
Zone 2	−50° to	−40°
Zone 3	−40° to	−30°
Zone 4	−30° to	−20°
Zone 5	−20° to	−10°
Zone 6	−10° to	0°
Zone 7	0° to	10°
Zone 8	10° to	20°
Zone 9	20° to	30°
Zone 10	30° to	40°

Achillea millefolium 'Fire King'

Alchemilla vulgaris

Varieties: *Acanthus mollis* 'Latifolius' has larger leaves and is hardier. It should be the choice for borderline areas in northern zone 8.

A. mollis 'Oak Leaf' has larger leaves that are more deeply cut.

Achillea filipendulina
(Fernleaf Yarrow)
Daisy family. Native to Asia Minor and the Caucasus.

The fernleaf yarrow is an easy perennial with ferny, soft-textured foliage and large clusters of tiny yellow flowers. Some excellent related species and varieties have flowers of white or rose.

The flower clusters are flat on top and are held on elongated stalks. Bloom peaks from late June to mid-July, and the season can be prolonged by removing spent blossoms.

The grayish foliage is dense almost to the ground and is effective all season. Growing 3 to 4 feet high, the plant is somewhat open and erect; but groups of three or more present a bushy appearance.

The plant is long-lived and does not spread inordinately. It occasionally self-sows, but the seedlings will produce inferior plants.

How to start: Divisions or nursery plants can be planted in early spring or fall. Named varieties may not come true from seed. Germinate indoors in February or March at 65° to 70°, and seeds will sprout in 5–7 days. Sow outdoors in early spring; seedlings will appear in 10–15 days.

Where to plant: Soil must be well drained, preferably dry, and of only average fertility: too rich soil promotes weak growth and few flowers. Give it full sun. Yarrow tolerates drought and poor, dry soil. Place it away from wind to reduce the need for staking. The plant is hardy in all zones.

Care: Easy. Water only moderately and avoid excessive nitrogen fertilizer. Powdery mildew and stem rot are occasional problems, especially in moist climates. Avoid watering late in the day. The plant requires division every 3 or 4 years to rejuvenate. It propogates easily from divisions, which should be taken in early fall or spring.

Related species and varieties: *Achillea filipendulina* 'Coronation Gold' is lower growing, to 2½ or 3 feet high, blooms most prolifically, and requires less staking.

A. f. 'Gold Plate' has huge flower clusters, up to 6 inches across, on tall, densely foliaged 4- to 5-foot plants.

A. f. 'Parkers Variety' has an open structure to 3½ feet high.

A. 'Moonshine' is low growing, to only 1½ feet tall, with silvery foliage and pale canary yellow flowers.

A. millefolium 'Fire King' is also only 1½ feet tall, with flowers that open whitish and change to a deep rosy red. Flower clusters are 2 to 3 inches across and leaves are more finely textured than other yarrows.

A. ptarmica 'Angels Breath' is 1 to 2 feet tall and produces great masses of tiny double white flowers. It can be extremely invasive, especially in moist, rich soil. Divide at least every other year to restrain its growth; it may even need this annually.

Alchemilla vulgaris
(Lady's Mantle)
Rose family. Native to Europe.

Delicate, fluffy flowers arch from the refined grayish-green leaves of this plant, which is useful in the front of the border or as a ground cover in partial shade.

The flowers are chartreuse or yellowish green in color and bloom in June through August. They appear on stalks up to 18 inches long that arch over the clump of foliage.

The leaves are 3 to 4 inches wide and rounded, with lobes creased like a fan. Slightly hairy, they catch droplets of water that sparkle in the sunlight. The foliage is effective all summer long.

Lady's mantle is long-lived and notoriously invasive, an advantage as a ground cover.

How to start: Plant divisions or nursery bedding plants in early spring or autumn. Sow seed indoors in early spring at 65°, or sow directly outdoors. Seeds germinate in 8 days.

Where to plant: The soil should be moist, well drained, and of average fertility. The plant prefers partial shade, especially in hot climates. Space plants 10 inches apart and plant in clumps of three or more. Hardy to zone 3.

Care: Easy. Keep moist. Remove spent flowers to prevent rampant spreading. There are no serious pests. The plant can go for many years without requiring division for rejuvenating or thinning. For increase, divide 3- or 4-year-old plants in autumn or early spring.

Anchusa azurea

Amsonia tabernaemontana

Amsonia tabernaemontana
(Blue Star; Amsonia)
Dogbane family. Native to the
Southeast United States.

The blue star is refined and delicate,
not the showiest perennial. Its clusters
of small stars are effective for only 2
weeks in late May and early June (although in northern climates it has been
known to bloom as late as July). The
willowlike foliage, however, is attractive
all summer long. The plant's chief advantage is perhaps that it is extremely
easy, restrained in growth, and carefree.

The flowers are an unusual steel
blue in color. Tiny and delicate, they
appear in dense clusters at the ends of
the stems.

The foliage is bright green all summer, turning brilliant gold in the fall.
The leaves are long, narrow, and medium fine in texture. The clumps of
multibranched stems are bushy and
semi-erect, growing 2 to 3 feet tall and
1½ to 2 feet wide. The plant is very
long-lived and grows slowly, never presenting a problem spreading about the
garden.

How to start: Plant divisions or nursery plants in the fall. It can be grown
from seed collected fresh and sown in
fall. If sown in spring, first pre-chill for
several weeks, then sow at 45°. Seeds
sprout in 3 weeks.

Where to plant: Blue star performs
well in nearly any soil, moist or dry, but
soggy soils should be avoided. It is best
in partial shade, but tolerates full sun
well. Space plants 12 to 15 inches apart.

Care: Extremely easy. The plant does
best with regular water and feeding. It
has no serious pests. Division is never
necessary, but it is an excellent means
of increase. Divide in spring or fall.

Anchusa azurea
(Italian Bugloss; Italian Alkanet)
Borage family. Native to the
Mediterranean region.

Although the Italian bugloss is a short-
lived plant, you can expect its clouds
of pure, vivid blue flowers to remain in
the garden for a long time; it is a prolific self-sower. Striking color is the only
reason for growing this plant, as its
foliage is coarse and unappealing.

The flowers bloom in June and most
of July. Individually they are tiny, but
are borne profusely in large, loose clusters on the top third of the plant.

The foliage is dark green with bristly,
hairy stems and leaves that become
quite rangy and unattractive after
blooming is complete. The plant is upright and spreading, with most foliage
at the base. It grows 3 to 5 feet tall.

Anchusa self-sows prolifically and can
become a nuisance. It is often treated
as a fall-sown annual or biennial, and
the flowers are best on 1- or 2-year old
plants.

How to start: Sow seed in late summer or early fall, or sow outdoors in
the spring at 50° to 65°. Start indoors 6
to 8 weeks prior to the last frost in
spring. Seedlings appear in 14 days.

Where to plant: Anchusa performs
well in nearly any soil, but is best in
well-drained, moist loam of average to
poor fertility. It prefers full sun but
tolerates partial shade. The tallest varieties should be located away from wind.
Plant 18 to 30 inches apart. Hardy to
zone 3.

Care: Moderately easy. Water plentifully, especially during drought. Do not
fertilize. Cut back after bloom to encourage a secondary (although usually
inferior) bloom. Tall varieties will require staking. Crown rot in soggy soils
is a serious problem.

Divide anchusa every year, or at least
every other year. Thin self-sown seedlings to avoid crowding.

Varieties: 'Dropmore' grows 4 to 5
feet tall with huge clouds of bright blue
flowers. It requires staking. 'Loddon
Royalist' reaches only 3 feet in height.
'Pride of Dover' reaches 4 feet with
lighter blue flowers, and requires staking. 'Royal Blue' has intense, deep blue
flowers and grows to a compact 3 feet
high.

Anemone × hybrida
(Japanese Anemone)
Buttercup family. Parents native to
China, Japan, and Nepal.

The Japanese anemone displays attractive foliage and loose, open clusters of
flowers in white and shades of pink.
It is especially valuable for providing
fall color in partial shade.

The flowers are each 1½ to 3 inches
across, depending on variety and conditions of growth, and bloom in late summer to mid-autumn.

The leaves are dark to light green,
large, deeply lobed, and pleasantly
coarse in texture. Reminiscent of maple
leaves, they are quite effective, especially during the bloom period. They
cover the plant densely at the bottom
and become smaller and more scarce
toward the top, leaving the upper 1 to
2 feet of stem bare. Japanese anemones
grow 2 to 5 feet tall.

Anemone × hybrida
with Crocosmia foliage in foreground

Anthemis tinctoria

Aquilegia hybrid

The plants slowly increase in size and number of flowering stems. They are well behaved, long-lived in favorable locations, and resent disturbance once established.

How to start: Commercially produced rooted cuttings should be purchased in individual containers and planted in spring. To plant your own cuttings, place 2-inch pieces of roots in sandy loam outdoors in early spring, and keep evenly moist.

Where to plant: Rich, moist soil high in humus. Soil must have sharp drainage; wet soil in winter is usually fatal. The plant prefers partial shade but tolerates full sun, especially in cool climates. Space plants 18 inches apart. Hardy to zone 6.

Care: Moderately easy. Water during dry spells in summer. In the northern limits of its hardiness range it is advisable to protect with a loose mulch, such as evergreen boughs. Do not apply this protection until the ground is frozen, however, or trapped moisture will lead to an early death. The black blister beetle can quickly defoliate established plants.

Clumps rarely require division. If necessary, divide in early spring; success is usually difficult. For increase, root cuttings are better.

Anthemis tinctoria
(Golden Marguerite)
Daisy family. Native to central and southern Europe and western Asia.

The golden marguerite produces masses of small golden yellow daisies on 2-foot bushy clumps in July. Although short-lived, it is useful in the border or for cut flowers.

The individual flowers are small, to 2 inches in diameter, but are massed in profusion on long, strong stems. The plant blooms in July, but removing spent flowers before they set seed can prolong the season into September.

The fernlike leaves are dark green on the upper surface, white and wooly on the undersides. They are medium fine in texture, aromatic when bruised, and effective all season long. The foliage is dense and bushy, and grows 2½ to 3 feet tall. The plant self-sows prolifically, and can become a nuisance.

How to start: Sow seed directly outdoors in spring or summer, or start indoors 6 to 8 weeks prior to setting seedlings out after the last frost in spring. Indoor germination will take from 1 to 3 weeks at 68° to 70°. The plant often can be purchased as divisions or rooted cuttings; plant these in spring or early summer.

Where to plant: Anthemis performs well in nearly any soil as long as it is well drained. Give it full sun. It tolerates hot, dry locations and poor soil remarkably well, but abhors heavy, wet, clay soils. Plant 15 to 18 inches apart. Hardy to zone 3.

Care: Moderately easy. Water only moderately. There are no serious pests. Anthemis must be divided every other year, at least, as clumps will die out in the center. Annual division may be required in moist climates. Divide in spring or fall.

Varieties: 'Moonlight' has pale yellow flowers; 'Beauty of Grallegh' has flowers of deep yellow; and 'E. C. Buxton' has very bright, yellow flowers.

Aquilegia
species and hybrids
(Columbine)
Buttercup family. Native to the cool northern temperate zones, mostly in North America and Europe.

Columbines are delicate, airy plants with curiously spurred, showy flowers in a wide range of colors and forms. They are useful in the border and in "wild" gardens.

The flowers come in shades of white, blue, purple, red, pink, yellow, orange, reddish brown, or nearly black, in solids or bicolors. They appear in May and June. Each bloom consists of five tubular petals that extend into spurs beyond the rear of the blossom, and of five sepals. Hybridizers have developed a huge array not only of color but of flower size, from 1½ to 4 inches across and up to 6 inches long. The flowers nod gracefully at the ends of long, slender stems.

The foliage is light green, often with a slight silvery, dusty cast that catches and holds dewdrops. Notched, compound leaves give the plant an open, finely textured appearance somewhat like that of maidenhair fern. Foliage can be effective into August if not attacked by leaf miners. The plant grows from 18 to 36 inches tall.

Columbine is usually short-lived, especially if the soil does not have perfect drainage. It does self-sow in favorable environments, but the offspring will differ, often radically, from hybrid parents.

Armeria maritima

Artemisia schmidtiana
'Silver Mound' with *Astilbe*

How to start: The plant can be started from seed, although young seedlings or divisions from a nursery are the usual methods. Sow seed outdoors in early spring or summer for flowers the next year. Or start indoors in a flat of sandy soil 12 to 14 weeks before setting out in mid-spring. Refrigerate the flat for 3 weeks, then put it in a moist, shady place at 70° to 75°. Do not cover the seeds, as indirect light is required for germination, which usually occurs in 3 to 4 weeks.

Where to plant: These are predominantly woodland plants and as such prefer cool, moist soil rich in organic matter. Drainage must be excellent. They prefer filtered shade, but will tolerate full sun in cool-summer climates, although this will tend to shorten the flowering period. Space plants 12 to 24 inches apart. Hardy to zone 3.

Care: Moderately difficult unless species are grown. Water generously and give regular light feedings, applying fertilizer at half strength. The chief pest problem is disfigurement of foliage by a leaf miner and by the columbine borer. Spray with malathion in early, middle, and late May, and carefully remove infected plants.

Division can be performed for increase in August and September; but it probably is best to keep new plants coming on by sowing fresh seed yearly. When dividing, break the clumps apart carefully and perform the operation quickly. Never allow the roots to dry out.

Armeria maritima
(Sea Pink; Sea Thrift)
Leadwort family. Native to the seacoasts of Europe, Asia Minor, and northern Africa.

The sea pink is a hardy evergreen perennial that forms dense cushions of grasslike foliage, from which arise small rounded flowers in colors of white or pale pink to deep rose. The plant is excellent for edging, rock gardens, cut flowers, and possibly for beds and borders.

The flowers appear in May and June, and sporadically the year round in mild climates. They are produced in dense, tiny heads about 1 inch in diameter, atop erect stems reaching 6 to 12 inches above the foliage.

The bright green, narrow leaves make a low, matlike mound 3 or 4 inches high; but size is quite variable from seed. The tufts of foliage gradually expand by short runners into clumps 1 to 1½ feet across. After about 4 years (sooner in overly moist locations) the center begins to die out, necessitating division.

How to start: Young plants are often purchased in flats or containers as divisions, but are easy to start from seed. Soak the seeds for several hours and then sow outdoors in spring or summer. Or start indoors for planting out in early summer, by sowing in a flat of sandy soil and maintaining a temperature of 65° to 70°. Germination occurs in 2 to 3 weeks.

Where to plant: Armeria must have excellent drainage, and will perform well in almost pure sand. It is best in dry, infertile soil and full sun. It tolerates perfectly constant wind and salt spray. Space plants 6 to 12 inches apart. Hardy to zone 3.

Care: Easy. Do not fertilize except in the poorest of soils, and then only lightly. Water only moderately. Excessive moisture and fertility hasten dying out in the center. Prolong bloom by judiciously removing faded flowers before they set seed. Do not mulch over winter or rot may result. The plant has no serious pests.

When the center of the clump begins to die, divide to rejuvenate. Division is an excellent means of increase, and can be performed in spring, summer, or fall.

Related species and varieties: Armeria is quite variable from seed and many cultivars are listed. Where uniformity of size or color is desired, it is best to choose a named variety.

A. plantaginea is like a large *A. maritima*, growing 1½ to 2 feet tall. Although it is less frequently available commercially, its larger size suits it better to the border. Like *A. maritima* it is extremely variable from seed. 'Bee's Ruby' has later, bright, deep red flowers in June and July.

Artemisia schmidtiana
'Silver Mound'
(Silver Mound; Wormwood; Angel's Hair)
Daisy family. Native to Japan.

The silver mound is famous for its intense silvery gray, feathery foliage produced in neat, dense mounds. It is perhaps the most popular gray-foliage accent plant.

The leaves are heavily divided, have a very soft, fine texture, and form a bushy, rounded mound 12 inches high and 18 inches wide. The flowers are inconspicuous.

Aruncus dioicus

Asclepias tuberosa

In perfect conditions the plant can be long-lived, but if the soil is over-moist, particularly during winter, it will not survive long. If soil is too rich, the foliage tends to become too lush and the plant will open at the center. It never spreads or reseeds.

How to start: Stem cuttings are easy to root during the summer; most nursery plants are started this way. Set young plants out in spring.

Where to plant: Silver mound must have perfect drainage; it will not tolerate soggy roots, especially in winter. Poor, dry, sandy soil and full sun are best. It tolerates heat, but is prone to rot in climates of excessive summer humidity. Space plants 18 to 24 inches apart. Hardy to zone 5.

Care: Easy. Avoid overwatering or fertilizing. Rust is the only serious pest, but fungicide is rarely required. Always water early in the day, and avoid letting water stand on the foliage for any length of time. Division is difficult, never necessary, and seldom successful.

Aruncus dioicus
formerly *A. sylvester*
(Goatsbeard)
Rose family. Native to Eurasia and North America.

Goatsbeard is a large, shrublike perennial that produces showy, silky white plumes in midsummer. The plant suggests a large astilbe, and is excellent in partial shade in the rear of the border or as a shrub accent, particularly in combination with astilbe and filipendula.

The flowers are minute and gathered into the gracefully relaxed plumes, which are often as long as 16 inches. They appear in mid-June to early July.

The foliage is medium green with large, compound leaves of bold texture. It is effective all season long. The plant is 5 to 7 feet tall, spreading 3 to 5 feet across. It is long-lived and, despite its large size, restrained in growth and not invasive.

How to start: Seeds sown at 45° in early spring will germinate in 2 weeks. Set container-grown plants out in early spring.

Where to plant: Moist, preferably rich soil high in organic matter. Aruncus is best grown in partial shade, such as under a high canopy of trees or on the east side of a building; but with sufficient moisture it tolerates full sun. Space plants 3 to 5 feet apart. Hardy to zone 4.

Care: Easy. Water generously and deeply. Fertilize regularly during the growing season. Despite its height, it never needs staking. It has no serious pests. The plant can go many years before needing division for rejuvenation. Division for increase is difficult and rarely successful.

Asclepias tuberosa
(Butterfly Flower; Butterfly Weed)
Milkweed family. Native from New England to North Dakota, south to Florida, Arizona, and New Mexico.

Brilliant orange-red clusters of flowers appear on this North American native in midsummer to attract hordes of butterflies, hummingbirds, and bees to the garden.

The flowers are most commonly found in deep orange; but varieties from pale lemon to deep oxblood red are becoming available. The individual blooms are tiny, but appear in many dense clusters at the ends of the stems.

They normally bloom from June to August, but peak from mid-June to early July. The milkweedlike fruits are attractive in dried arrangements.

The lance-shape leaves are dark green and hairy. Each plant is composed of a cluster of erect stems branched toward the top, giving it an erect and slightly spreading form. It grows from 18 to 36 inches tall. The plant is restrained in growth and long-lived. Its deep tap root promotes drought tolerance but renders it difficult to divide or transplant.

How to start: It is best to plant the tuberous bare roots when the plant is dormant in the fall or early spring. Set the bare tap root vertically into the soil so that the "eye" is 1 to 2 inches below the soil line. Seed-starting is possible, but germination is erratic and unpredictable. Sow seeds outdoors in May or indoors in early spring at 68° to 75°. Seedlings appear in 3 to 4 weeks.

Where to plant: Native to meadows and prairies, asclepias is best in light, sandy, poor soil and full sun. Expect good performance in peaty soil or even heavy clay. Avoid excessively moist soils. It tolerates wind. Space plants 12 to 18 inches apart. Hardy to zone 3.

Care: Easy. Water only through drought, especially in heavy soils. It is slow to appear in the spring, so take care when cultivating around its area. There are no serious pests. Division is never necessary, and is difficult and rarely successful.

Aster hybrid

Astilbe hybrid

Aster
species and hybrids
(Hardy Aster; Michaelemas Daisy)
Daisy family. The parents of many
hybrids are native to North America,
Europe, and Asia.

Familiar for their late-season color, asters produce daisylike flowers in late
summer and fall, in all shades except
orange. Many varieties are available for
flower color and size. Although requiring frequent division, they are easy to
grow.

The flowers are usually violet-purple
or blue, but many shades of purple,
red, pink, and white are also available.
All have yellow centers. They are about
2 inches across and are produced in
large clusters at the ends of the stems,
blooming any time from August into
October, depending upon variety.

The foliage is dark to dusty green
and of medium-coarse texture. Leaves
are hairy, sticky, and linear or lance-
shape. Low-growing varieties are bushy,
prostrate, and spreading, creating
dense carpets of color as low as 9
inches. Taller varieties range from 18
inches to 6 feet high, and their clusters
of erect stems are heavily branched
toward the top and densely covered
with foliage.

The aster form is generally upright
and spreading. Clumps increase quickly
and begin to die out in the center at
an early age, necessitating division. The
plant reseeds sporadically, but the hybrids will not breed true to type. It is
fairly short-lived without adequate
maintenance.

How to start: Named varieties are
best started by divisions, nursery plants,
or hand-pollinated seed. Divisions of
young plants are best set out in early
spring. Sow seed outdoors in spring or
early summer, or indoors in early

spring. Sow thickly, as the percentage
of germination is usually low. Seedlings
appear in 2 to 3 weeks at 70° to 75°.

Where to plant: Asters are not too
particular about soil, but light, moist,
well-drained soil of average fertility
is best. They accept full sun or partial
shade, preferring the latter in hot
southern climates. Space plants 12 to
20 inches apart. Hardy to zone 4.

Care: Moderately easy to moderately
difficult. The plant performs best with
abundant water, but never allow roots
to remain soggy. Feed only lightly.
Pinch in late spring to produce better
flowering and denser plants. Varieties
over 2 feet tall will need support to
protect them from wind and rain; the
recommended method of staking is
to provide twiggy branches the plants
can grow up and around.

Rust and powdery mildew can be serious; so protect plants throughout
the growing season with a weekly spraying of fungicide. Do not let moisture
stand on foliage in cool weather or in
the evening. Japanese beetles can also
be a problem, particularly on earlier-
blooming varieties. Later-blooming
flowers usually open after the beetle
season has run its course.

Division is necessary at least every
other year, and often annually, as
clumps start dying out in the center.
Division is an excellent means of increase and should be done in early
spring.

Related species and varieties:
Aster × frikartii 'Wonder of Stafa' is the
best choice for the hot, humid summers
of the Southeast. Its lavender-blue
flowers, sometimes appearing as early
as June, are effective well into October.
It is marginally hardy in southern zone
6. Mulch well in the northern limits of
its range to protect over winter. It
grows 2½ feet tall and requires staking.

Astilbe
species and hybrids
(False Spirea; Astilbe)
Saxifrage family. Native to eastern Asia.

Astilbe is a favorite perennial for shady,
moist locations, and also performs well
in full sun. It offers glossy, dark green
foliage and fluffy plumes of white,
pink, lavender, or red flowers on erect
or arching stems. The tiny flowers are
produced in great quantities and the
effect is delicate and feathery. It blooms
in June and July.

The leaves are divided and compound. Sometimes tinged with bronze,
they resemble a coarse fern and are
always lush and refined. The foliage
forms bushy mounds rarely exceeding
1 or 2 feet in height; the flowers often
reach another 12 to 18 inches more.
Most flower heads are erect and pyra-
midical; others arch gracefully.

Astilbe will gradually spread as
clumps expand. Being a heavy feeder,
it will deplete the soil and flower less as
years go by; but division every 3 or 4
years will rejuvenate the flowering. The
plant is restrained in growth, not invasive, and long-lived.

How to start: Divisions or nursery
plants are best set out in spring. Nurseries frequently offer young container-
grown plants. Seed is difficult to germinate and displays radical variability.

Where to plant: A cool, moist location in light shade, with deep, rich soil
high in organic matter. It does not tolerate wet winters well without adequate
drainage, and will not take summer
drought. It performs well in deep
shade but accepts full sun if watered
deeply and often. Space plants 1 to
2 feet apart. Hardy to zone 4.

Aurinia saxatilis

Baptisia australis

Belamcanda chinensis

Care: Moderately easy. Give generous applications of 5–10–10 fertilizer each spring just as growth begins. Water abundantly. Japanese beetles can be a serious pest. Powdery mildew, slugs, and snails also can be problems. Although the plant will perform adequately without division, for maximum flower size and quantity it is best to divide every 3 or 4 years. It is easy to propagate by dividing the root stock just as plants are beginning to grow in the spring.

Aurinia saxatilis
formerly *Alyssum saxatile*
(Basket-of-Gold; Goldentuft)
Mustard family. Native to southern and central Europe and Turkey.

The basket-of-gold is a low, bushy perennial of variable habit, covered with bright lemon yellow flowers in April and May. Useful in dry, poor soil, it is frequently grown in rock gardens.

Individually the flowers are tiny, but they are produced in incredible profusion, entirely covering the plant. The foliage is gray green, providing an interesting accent when the plant is not in bloom. The leaves are small, elongated, and cover the plant densely.

The form varies according to the selected variety and to growth conditions. In rich, moist soil it tends to be open and sprawling; in dry, poor soil it will be compact and bushy, 9 to 12 inches high and spreading to 12 or 15 inches. It is fairly short-lived.

How to start: Plant divisions or nursery plants in early spring. Or sow seed outdoors in early spring. Seedlings appear in 1 to 2 weeks.

Where to plant: Dry, poor, infertile soil in full sun is preferred, and drainage must be excellent. Plant 8 to 12 inches apart. Hardy to zone 3.

Care: Water only moderately through periods of drought. Do not fertilize. After blooming is over, cut the stems to half their length to keep the plant vigorous. It has no serious pests. Divide to increase in spring just as growth commences.

Baptisia australis
(False Indigo)
Pea family. Native to Pennsylvania, south to North Carolina and Tennessee.

False indigo is a large perennial with mildly showy spikes of flowers in late spring. Hardy, pest-free, and undemanding, this is one of the easiest perennials to grow. It is excellent for backgrounds and at the rear of the border, or as a shrublike mass in the landscape.

The flowers are often described as "indigo blue," but actually range from pale lavender to dark purple. They are pea-shape, about 1 inch long, and are produced in long, erect spikes at the top of the branches, appearing in late May to early June.

The foliage is dense, lush, and remains attractive until hard frost in the fall. The cloverlike leaves are a clean, bright green, and divided into three leaflets.

False indigo forms shrubby, rounded masses 3 or 4 feet tall, sometimes taller, and spreads as wide. It is restrained in growth, will not spread, and is long-lived.

How to start: Best from young nursery plants. It is easy to grow from seed sown outdoors in late fall or early spring, but it will not begin to flower

for 2 or 3 years. Propagating from division is difficult.

Where to plant: Best in well-drained garden loam of average fertility. It tolerates nearly any soil but very wet ones. Give it full sun or partial shade, although flowering will be reduced in shade. Plant 18 to 24 inches apart. Hardy to zone 3.

Care: Extremely easy. The tallest plants may require staking to prevent breakage in high winds. Remove spent flowers to prolong bloom. (However, the black, long-lasting seed pods are considered attractive by many.) As a legume, it "fixes" its own nitrogen from the atmosphere, and needs little if any feeding. It prefers poor soil. Water only moderately.

Although powdery mildew and rust are reported, they are seldom serious problems. Division is extremely difficult due to the deep tap root, and is seldom successful. Luckily, it is not necessary either for rejuvenation or propagation.

Belamcanda chinensis
(Blackberry Lily; Leopard Flower)
Iris family. Native to China and Japan.

The blackberry lily produces great quantities of star-shape flowers in late July and August. Orange in color with red dots, they measure about 2 inches across and appear on multibranched stems that can reach as high as 4 feet. The clusters of seeds that follow resemble blackberries, and are attractive in dried arrangements.

The swordlike leaves are bright green to gray green and resemble those of tall bearded iris. They form large clumps of foliage 2 to 3 feet high.

Bergenia cordifolia

Brunnera macrophylla

Blackberry lily may reseed, but the seedlings are easy to weed out. The clumps expand slowly and the plant is long-lived.

How to start: Easy to start from seed, but faster results occur from nursery plants or tubers divided and planted in the spring.

Where to plant: Belamcanda must have well-drained soil, as winter sogginess is usually fatal. Give it full sun. Space plants 1 to 3 feet apart. The plant is best used, however, as a single specimen. Hardy to zone 5.

Care: Easy in well-drained soil. In northern areas it should have a protective layer of loose mulch over winter. Iris borer can be a severe pest. See *Iris* (Bearded Iris) for recommendations. While division is an excellent method for increase, clumps can go for many years without needing it for rejuvenation. Division is best performed in the spring or early fall.

Related species: *Belamcanda flabellata* is similar in all respects except that the flowers are clear yellow and bloom slightly later, into September. It is less commonly available.

Bergenia cordifolia
and hybrids
(Bergenia; Heart-Leaf Bergenia)
Saxifrage family. Native to Siberia and Mongolia.

Bergenia is a low-growing evergreen perennial with large, rounded, cabbage-like leaves and pink or white flowers. Undemanding, adaptable to nearly any situation, and extremely hardy, it is useful in the front of the border or massed as a bed or ground cover.

The flowers are about 3/4 inch wide and appear in clusters atop stems extending 6 to 12 inches above the foliage. They bloom in April and May normally, but may not appear in areas of severe winters or other harsh exposure.

The foliage is medium green in summer, with a reddish tinge in winter. Leaves are wavy-edged, fleshy, and measure 10 inches across, radiating in all directions from the base.

Measuring 12 to 15 inches high, the plant spreads by rhizomes that creep along the soil surface, to form dense mats of leaves. In excessively fertile situations it may leave bare spots as the clump expands. It grows slowly and could never be called invasive.

How to start: While best started from divisions in early spring, it also can be raised from seed sown outdoors in late fall or early spring.

Where to plant: Bergenia tolerates a wide variety of soils, performing well in poor, dry ones and rich, moist ones; but it prefers well-drained soil of average fertility. More frequent division is necessary in rich, moist soil. Give it either sun or shade. The latter is better in regions of hot summers. Space plants 12 to 18 inches apart. Hardy to zone 2.

Care: Easy. It responds vigorously to fertilizing, but this will also result in stretching, bare spots, and the need for more frequent division. Water only moderately for the same reason. It has no serious pests, but does provide a haven for snails. On dry sites with relatively infertile soil, it will not need division for years. In rich, moist soil it may need it about every 4 years.

Brunnera macrophylla
(Siberian Bugloss)
Borage family. Native to the Caucasus and western Siberia.

The tiny flowers of Siberian bugloss, produced in delicate clusters, resemble those of *Anchusa azurea*, the Italian bugloss. This plant, however, has the advantage of excellent, large, heart-shape leaves that remain attractive all season long. In addition, it is easy and adaptable whether grown in full sun or shade.

The flower color is a clear sky blue, and blooms appear generously in branching, open clusters atop stems 12 to 15 inches tall. They bloom in April through May and somewhat resemble forget-me-nots.

The dark green leaves are clean, lush, and pest-free. They reach 6 to 8 inches long in July and grow in basal clumps about 12 inches high. The foliage is effective until frost.

The plant expands outward gradually. It is well behaved, not invasive, and lives a long time without requiring division.

How to start: By clump divisions taken in early spring, by nursery plants, or by seed sown outdoors in early fall. To sow seed in spring, freeze for 1 week to break dormancy; then sow in early spring at 45°. Germination takes 2 weeks.

Where to plant: Exceedingly adaptable, the plant performs well in any soil, in sun or shade. Like most garden plants, however, it responds to a moist soil high in organic matter. Partial shade is best. Space plants 12 to 18 inches apart. Hardy to zone 3.

Care: Easy. It is best with abundant water and regular feeding, but does well with little attention. It has no seri-

Caltha palustris 'Flore Pleno'

Campanula carpatica

Ceratostigma plumbaginoides

ous pests. Division is needed if the center begins to die out, but this rarely occurs before many years.

Caltha palustris
(Marsh Marigold)
Buttercup family. Native to Eurasia and North America from Alaska to North Carolina.

The marsh marigold is a cheerful little plant for wet, soggy soil or standing water. It has bright golden yellow flowers about 1 inch across borne singly above the foliage. The bright green, rounded leaves are held horizontally on tall, juicy stems. A spring bloomer (May), the entire plant disappears by midsummer.

The plant is fairly low growing, from 12 to 18 inches high. Although not considered invasive, it will expand to form loose clumps and mats. It reseeds if conditions are favorable.

How to start: Divisions and nursery plants are best. To grow from seed, sow only fresh seed in pots, plunge in water, then keep surface evenly moist. Plants bloom the third year from seed.

Where to plant: Rich soil high in organic matter and with a constant moisture supply is best. With abundant watering the plant will tolerate drier soils. It grows happily in marshy areas or standing water. Give it full sun or very light shade. Plant 12 to 24 inches apart. Hardy to zone 3.

Care: Moderately easy to moderately difficult. Water abundantly and fertilize regularly. Mulch well if it is planted in exposed, dry locations. There are no serious pests. Divide to increase just after blooming is over. The plant can go for years without needing division.

Campanula persicifolia
(Peach-Leaf Bellflower)
Harebell family. Native to Europe and Northeast Asia.

The blue or white blossoms of the peach-leaf bellflower are a charming addition to any wild garden or informal border.

The flowers are bell shape, single or double, and spread open to 1½ inches in diameter. They appear in July on long, slender, flexible stems.

The leaves are medium green and straplike, and, as indicated by the common name, are similar to those of the peach tree.

The plant spreads outward gradually. It is restrained in growth, not invasive, and can be quite long-lived.

How to start: Best from nursery plants or clumps divided in early spring. It also starts easily from seed sown outdoors in early spring or late summer; however, seeds seldom produce plants true to type, and considerable variation may result.

Where to plant: As bellflower is native to mountainous meadows and open woods, the soil must be well drained, and should be high in organic matter and of average fertility. Give the plant full sun or partial shade. It is best in areas with cool summers, and does not perform well in the South. Space plants 12 to 18 inches apart. Hardy to zone 3.

Care: Easy. Water regularly, as it does not tolerate prolonged drought. Feed lightly and infrequently. The tallest varieties may require staking, although this is unusual.

Crown rot can be a serious problem if water stands around the roots for any length of time. Regular applications of insecticide may be beneficial in protecting the plants from aphids and thrips.

Divide to rejuvenate when the clumps begin to decline, usually not before the third or fourth year. Division in early spring is an excellent means of increase.

Related species: Campanula carpatica (Carpathian Harebell) is a low, 6- to 12-inch-high plant with large blue, purple, or white blossoms from June to August. It is neat, compact, and long-blooming, and is useful in the rock garden, in the front of the border, or as an edging. Protect from slugs.

C. glomerata (Clustered Bellflower) has very showy, large, tight clusters of violet, blue, purple, or white flowers atop erect stems. Give this plant full sun only, as in shady situations it tends to spread invasively by runners. It flowers in June and July.

Ceratostigma plumbaginoides
(Blue Plumbago)
Leadwort family. Native to western Asia.

The blue plumbago is a low-growing, leafy perennial with brilliant gentian blue flowers in late summer. Its late-season blue makes it an excellent choice for beds, edging, and the front of the border.

The flowers are bright blue upon opening and change to violet as they age. They appear in great quantities over the surface of the plant from August to frost.

The dark green leaves often turn a bronzy red in cool fall weather. Foliage is dense and of medium to fine texture. Growing 6 to 10 inches high, the plant can spread to 18 inches, sometimes more. Masses of slender, almost prostrate stems radiate from the center,

Chrysanthemum
'Seventh Heaven'

Chrysanthemum 'Loyalty'

Chrysanthemum
'Charms'

sending up many short vertical stems, each bearing flowers.

The plant spreads slowly by underground stems; in sand, the spread is rapid. It is long-lived and not invasive. Division is rarely required. Growth is slow to appear in spring; so early cultivation should be careful.

How to start: Transplant nursery plants or clumps divided in early spring.

Where to plant: Although not too particular about soil, the plant does best in well-drained, moist soil high in

organic matter. Avoid excessively soggy or dry soils. Give it full sun or partial shade. It is highly tolerant of drought. Space plants 12 to 18 inches apart. It is hardy to zone 6, but performs well in zone 5 with a light winter mulch.

Care: It requires little attention but will respond to abundant moisture and regular fertilizing. It has no serious pests. It rarely needs division, but clumps may start to die out in the center after 3 or 4 years. This is easily corrected by division. Best performed in early spring, division is also an excellent means of increase.

Chrysanthemum
hybrids
(Hardy Chrysanthemum)
Daisy family. Of hybrid origin.

Difficult to raise well, hardy chrysanthemums nevertheless can provide an outstanding show when nearly all other perennials have gone to bed for the winter. The plants offer an incredible variety of colors, sizes, and flower shapes. For the gardener with patience and attention to detail, they can yield extraordinary late-season dividends.

Flowers come in all colors except blue. Most varieties are fully double, with two flowers 2 to 4 inches across (and usually larger with disbudding, described later in the entry), produced alone or in clusters at the ends of branched stems. Many forms are available, some of which are described here:

Decorative chrysanthemums have fully double flowers with straplike "petals," or, more accurately, rays.

Pompons produce rounded, almost spherical flowers usually 2 inches or less across.

Singles are daisylike with an outer single or double row of rays and an often contrasting central eye.

Cushions usually have double flowers and are distinguished by their low, bushy habit, rarely exceeding 15 inches in height.

Spoons are odd-shaped flowers with long rays flaring out into spoonlike tips.

Commercials are reserved largely for greenhouse growers, and are characterized by the popular, huge "football game" flowers.

Anemones have contrasting outer rays and inner, fluffy eyes.

Buttons are like tiny pompons an inch or less across.

Rayonettes have a spidery, open quality with long, filamentous rays. They are often called "Spider Mums."

Hardy chrysanthemums bloom anytime from August to November, depending upon variety, and may bloom to December in mild climates.

The plant's overall structure differs with varieties, but generally is a cluster of many-branched stems. Forms range from the low, spreading cushion mums to tall, narrow upright ones. Heights range from 1 to 4 feet. The foliage is deep green, usually dense, and attractive all season long unless damaged by pests.

The plants gradually expand outward by sending up new shoots. They are restrained in growth, never invasive, and can be long-lived if properly cared for.

How to start: Division or stem cuttings made in late spring are the accepted methods. Do not set out young plants too early if a tall habit is not desired.

Where to plant: Rich, fertile soil high in organic matter is best; and it is critical that the soil be perfectly drained

Chrysanthemum
'John Hughs'

Chrysanthemum coccineum
'E. M. Robinson'

in winter. Once established, the plants can withstand mild drought. They flower best in full sun, but usually accept partial shade well. Space plants 18 to 24 inches apart. Hardy to zone 6, and possibly zone 5 if soil is very well drained in winter.

Care: Difficult for best appearance. Tip-pinching from spring to midsummer results in bushier, more heavily flowered plants. Start when the spring growth reaches about 6 inches, and continue each time it grows another 6 inches until mid-to-late July. Tall plants may need staking at flowering time. Feed regularly and generously throughout the growing season. Water regularly, especially over dry periods. Protect over winter with a 3- or 4-inch cover of mulch, placed after the ground is completely frozen, as the shallow roots are susceptible to frost heave. But guard against moisture collecting under the mulch, especially during thaws. Chrysanthemums will rot quickly in soggy, cold soil. To achieve fewer but larger flowers, often for show, gardeners practice disbudding. Remove all but four or five of the strongest stems in each clump, and when fewer buds begin to show, pinch off all except the one at the top.

A wide range of bacterial, fungal, viral, and insect pests can attack the plants. Regular spraying with an all-purpose spray (containing both insecticide and fungicide) and practicing good garden sanitation are essential for healthy plants. Carefully remove and destroy any plants infected with aster yellows, foliar nematodes, and stunting (a viral disease).

Most varieties require annual division to retain vigor and good appearance, although some can get by with division every other year. This is best done in spring.

Chrysanthemum coccineum
(Pyrethrum; Painted Daisy)
Daisy family. Native to Southwest Asia.

The painted daisy is much easier to cultivate than the hardy chrysanthemum and blooms earlier, from June to early July. It offers daisylike flowers in intense hues of pink, white, and red, often with a contrasting eye.

The flowers are 2 to 3 inches across, and are produced at the ends of long stems. They may be single or double.

The bright green, deeply dissected leaves are finely textured but relatively sparse. Stems are upright to spreading, frequently branched, and range in height from 9 inches to 3 feet, depending upon variety.

Painted daisies form clumps that gradually increase by sending up new shoots on the outer perimeter of the crown. They are long-lived and not invasive.

How to start: By division in late summer.

Where to plant: Reasonably well-drained soil high in organic matter. A rich, sandy loam is best. They will not tolerate wet soil in winter. Give them full sun or very light shade. Space plants 12 to 18 inches apart. Hardy to zone 2.

Care: Moderately easy. Painted daisies tolerate moderate drought, but do best with sufficient water. They seldom need staking. Cut all stems to the ground after flowering to encourage a secondary bloom in late summer. There are no serious pests. Division usually is necessary to relieve crowding after the fourth year, and is best done in late summer. After dividing and transplanting the clump, trim the leaves in half to reduce wilting. Division is an excellent means of increase.

Chrysanthemum parthenium
(Feverfew; Matricaria)
Daisy family. Native to southeastern Europe and the Caucasus.

Tiny daisylike flowers in incredible profusion cover these low, bushy plants in July and August. White with yellow centers, the blooms come in single- and double-flowered forms, although the single forms usually will self-sow invasively.

The flowers measure from ½ to ¾ inch in diameter and appear at the ends of multibranched stems. The leaves are light green, small, and dense. In mild climates the foliage is evergreen.

Feverfew is a low, spreading plant. Most named varieties grow 12 to 15 inches high. Seedlings can, however, eventually reach 3 feet and sprawl in an open fashion, unless pinched or sheared early in the season. Single-flower forms will self-sow everywhere; the double-flower varieties are less prolific. The species is quite long-lived, unlike the double-flower cultivars.

How to start: Seeds sown in spring will produce flowering plants that summer. It is also easy to grow by cuttings or divisions. In fact, the smallest piece of root taken inadvertently by a spade will start a new (sometimes unwanted) plant.

Where to plant: Feverfew tolerates many soils but performs best in sandy, well-drained loam. Give it full sun, although it is quite tolerant of partial shade. Space plants 12 to 24 inches apart. Hardy to zone 4.

Chrysanthemum × superbum 'Marconi'

Chrysanthemum parthenium,
double variety

Care: Easy, except for removing unwanted seedlings. Pinch in spring to produce denser, bushier plants. The reseeding problem tempts one to try removing flowers before they can set seed, but this is nearly impossible, as there are so many blossoms, and new ones are always appearing while others are setting seed. The plant has no serious pests. Division is seldom if ever required for rejuvenation, but is good for propagation in early spring.

Chrysanthemum × superbum
(Shasta Daisy)
Daisy family. Of hybrid origin; the parents probably native to Portugal and the Pyrenees.

White, daisylike flowers with a contrasting yellow eye generously cover this bushy plant all summer long.

The blossoms are 2 to 3 inches across and are produced in great profusion at the ends of strong stems. They bloom from June to frost. Single and double varieties are available.

The dark green leaves are narrow, toothed, and almost linear in shape. About an inch long, they are held close to the stem, presenting a fine texture. The plant is densely branched, rounded, and bushy, growing 2 to 4 feet high and as wide. The foliage will often persist well into winter; and the plant is often grown as an evergreen perennial in mild climates, where it tends to become woody at the base.

The Shasta daisy is restrained in growth and can be long-lived if located and cared for correctly.

How to start: Best planted as a nursery plant or division in spring. Sowing seed in spring is possible, and easy, but will result in considerable variation in plants.

Where to plant: Moist, fertile, very well-drained soil is best. It will not tolerate soggy soil in winter. Provide good air circulation and either full sun or partial shade. The double varieties show a distinct preference for partial shade in hot climates. Space plants 12 to 24 inches apart. Hardy to zone 5.

Care: Moderately easy. Water generously, especially during drought. It responds favorably to occasional feeding. Removing spent flowers will encourage a heavier bloom. Leaf spot, stem rot, verticillium rot, and several chewing insects can be troublesome. Plants attacked by verticillium rot should be carefully removed and destroyed. Division usually is necessary every other year to restore vigor. It is best done in the spring.

Chrysogonum virginianum
(Golden Star)
Daisy family. Native from Pennsylvania to Florida and Louisiana.

Golden star is a low, trailing plant with small, daisylike, bright yellow flowers and vivid green leaves. It is useful either in sun or shade, and is particularly delightful when grown against or around rocks.

The flowers appear in mid-June to frost and are produced along the joints of trailing, leafy stems. The bright green leaves are small and round, about an inch across, and are densely produced. Most varieties sold commercially have gray-green foliage.

The plant has a loose, open habit that follows the contour of the ground and rocks. It usually grows 2 to 4 inches high, and rarely exceeds 8 inches. It often spreads into a loose mat with stems rooting where they touch the soil. Golden star is always restrained in growth and never intrusive, seldom exceeding a spread of 12 to 20 inches.

How to start: Best started in early spring from divisions or nursery container plants. It is possible to start from seed sown in late spring or late summer, but expect considerable variation in leaf size and leaf color.

Where to plant: Chrysogonum must have excellent drainage and preferably a sandy soil high in organic matter. Give it either full sun or partial shade. The soil should be fairly dry and of only average fertility. Space plants 8 to 12 inches apart.

Care: Moderately easy. Removing spent flowers before they can set seed will prolong bloom. Water moderately during periods of drought. There are no serious pests. Divide in early spring for increase. The plant rarely if ever requires division for rejuvenation.

Cimicifuga racemosa
(Black Snakeroot; Bugbane)
Buttercup family. Native from Massachusetts to Ontario, south to Georgia, Tennessee, and Missouri.

The black snakeroot produces tall, thin, exceedingly graceful spires of white, fluffy flowers, sometimes reaching to 8 feet above the foliage clumps. It is excellent in the rear of the border.

Open and airy in bloom, the wand-like flower stalks sway with each breeze. The flowers are small and are produced densely along the upper part of the stalks, in racemes up to 3 feet long.

Chrysogonum virginianum

They are vertical and graceful, and exude a cloying sweet fragrance. The peak bloom occurs in late June and July, but small lateral branches bear flowers into August.

The glistening dark green leaves are compound, divided into three toothed leaflets. The foliage forms dense clumps 2 to 3 feet high and provides good color until frost.

Black snakeroot does not self-sow freely or spread about the garden, and can never be considered intrusive. The rhizomes expand slowly to increase the clump. The plant is very long-lived.

How to start: Division in early spring or container-grown nursery plants with well-developed root systems are best. To plant a bare-root clump from a division, place the rhizome (one with at least two eyes) so that the eyes are exactly 1 inch below soil level. Seeds may be collected and sown in the fall. To sow in spring, pre-chill in the refrigerator for several weeks. Sow at 45° to 50°. Germination is slow and erratic.

Where to plant: Since the plant is native to the deep, rich, moist soils of open woodlands and the forest edge, it is best in moist, well-drained soil high in organic matter. It grows tallest in deep soil and filtered shade, and ideally should not have more than 4 hours of direct sun each day. In deep shade, however, it will not flower well. Hardy to zone 3.

Care: Moderately easy. Water abundantly and fertilize regularly. The plant prefers cool soil, and it is best to mulch deeply throughout the summer. Division is an excellent means of increase, but is rarely required for rejuvenation. Clumps can go for many years left alone.

Related species: *Cimicifuga americana* is native to North America. Its foliage is more open and appears higher up the stalks. A smaller species, growing 2 to 4 feet tall, it blooms from August into September or October.

C. dahurica is native to Asia. Its foliage is more coarse, and it never exceeds 4 or 5 feet in height. It blooms from August into fall.

C. foetida (sometimes listed as *C. simplex*) is more branched at the base, grows from 18 to 36 inches high, and blooms in September and October.

Coreopsis lanceolata
(Perennial Coreopsis)
Daisy family. Native from Michigan south to Florida and New Mexico.

This perennial coreopsis produces bright golden yellow "daisies" on long stems above tufted, leafy mounds all summer long. They are most useful at the front or middle of the border.

The flowers have yellow "petals," actually ray flowers, with yellow or brown centers. They are about 3 inches wide and are produced in abundance on long stems in June through September.

The dark green leaves are long and straplike. The basal mounds, or tufts, of leaves support many flower stalks reaching to 2 feet high.

Although it often reseeds, perennial coreopsis is seldom invasive like its annual cousins. It is long-lived, and the clumps expand slowly from the center. Do not confuse this plant with several cultivars hybridized with *Coreopsis grandiflora*, as those are short-lived biennials.

How to start: Easy to start from seed, and most cultivars will breed true to type. Sow outdoors in spring or summer up to 2 months prior to the first frost; or, for flowers the first year, sow

Cimicifuga racemosa
with *Achillea* and *Echinops*

indoors 6 to 8 weeks ahead of the last frost in spring. Keep the germinating medium at 60° to 70°, and do not cover the seeds. The plant is also easy to start by clump division in spring.

Where to plant: The plant is extremely tolerant; give it any well-drained soil in full sun. Space them 12 inches apart. Hardy to zone 3.

Care: Easy. Water through dry periods and feed occasionally. For the longest bloom period, and to prevent reseeding, remove faded flowers before they can set seed. Leaf spot, rust, and powdery mildew can be severe problems. Foliage may also require protection from several chewing insects. While clumps can go for many years before requiring division to rejuvenate, it is an excellent means of increase in early spring.

Coreopsis verticillata 'Golden Shower'

Delphinium elatum

Related species: *Coreopsis grandiflora* is a short-lived biennial and a weedy self-sower. It has a shorter bloom season, from mid-June through July.

C. verticillata (Threadleaf Coreopsis) is full, bushy, and grows to 3 feet tall. Its dense foliage is exceedingly fine in texture, misty, and soft in appearance. The plant is covered with small golden flowers all summer. While not invasive, it performs best with frequent division. Of all coreopsis it is the most tolerant of dry soils. Threadleaf coreopsis is easy, restrained in growth, and long-lived.

Delphinium elatum
and hybrids
(Delphinium)
Buttercup family. Native from southern and central Europe to Siberia.

Famous for their tall, bold spikes in rich blues, delphiniums are a tricky flower to cultivate well. Much frustration has resulted from seeing pictures of these magnificent plants as raised in England, for there are not many areas of this country so conducive to their good growth. When grown well, however, they are rivaled by few flowers for their dramatic effect at the rear of the border.

The flowers are mostly blue, but also come in pink, white, red, violet, and purple. Individually they are spurred and solid or often bicolored, with a contrasting white or black eye, sometimes called a "bee." Borne profusely and densely along tall, vertical spikes, they bloom from June into July.

The dark green leaves are lobed and medium-coarse in texture. They are large and dense at the base, smaller and more scarce higher up. The stiffly erect stems appear in clumps and are

usually about 4 feet tall; under optimum conditions, however, they can reach 7 or 8 feet or more in height. Size also varies according to variety. The flowers are produced along the upper third or fourth of each stem, in dense vertical spikes.

Delphiniums are usually short-lived, often being treated as a biennial or a short-lived perennial. Under the best conditions, the clumps will expand gradually and the stems will grow in height and number as the years progress.

How to start: The most successful method is to start from container-grown plants purchased from the nursery either in early spring or early fall. Or start from divisions made in early spring, being sure to dust all cut surfaces with a fungicide. Avoid planting young starts or divisions too deeply. The plant can be started by seed sown outdoors in spring or summer. Or sow indoors, completely covered, at a temperature of 55° to 65°.

Where to plant: Soil must be rich, moist, well drained, and high in organic matter. It should be slightly alkaline, or at least neutral. Provide full sun and good air circulation. Originally native to the cool mountain meadows of Europe to Siberia, delphiniums will decline rapidly in regions with hot, muggy summers. Space plants 18 to 36 inches apart. Hardy to zone 2.

Care: Difficult, but the effort is worthwhile. Fertilize with a 5–10–10 fertilizer in early spring and again later during the growing season. Water abundantly but never let the soil remain soggy; and try not to get any moisture on the leaves. Staking is absolutely necessary to prevent the heavy spikes from breaking in the wind, and the shallow-rooted plants from dislodging from the soil. Because the roots are

shallow and delicate, cultivate gently. As blooms fade, snip off the spike just below the lowest blossom. When the new growth from the base reaches 6 inches, cut the old stem clear to the ground. This will produce a second, though less spectacular, bloom season in late summer.

Powdery mildew, crown rot, and several other fungal pests are problems, as are many insects, snails, and slugs. Applying both a fungicide and an insecticide at 10-day intervals is strongly advised. Remove and destroy all infected plants, and do not replant in the same area where crown rot has attacked. Protect the crowns from snails and slugs in fall and early spring. Mulch well after the ground freezes.

In favorable locations where they live long, delphiniums should be divided after every third or fourth year. This is best done in early spring just as the new growth appears. Dust all cut surfaces with fungicide.

Related species: *Delphinium belladonna* is a shorter species and is much longer-lived.

Dianthus plumarius
species and hybrids
(Cottage Pink; Scotch Pink)
Pink family. Native to central Europe.

Cottage pinks produce rose, pink, red, or white blossoms in spring on tufted, compact plants. Their gray-green leaves often persist through winter.

The flowers are about 1½ inches wide, fringed and lacy, and can be solid or bicolored, single or double. They appear in great quantities above the narrow, grasslike foliage, blooming in May and June.

The foliage forms dense mats 6 to 8 inches high, and the flower stems ex-

Dianthus plumarius

Dicentra spectabilis

tend the height to a total of 12 inches. The mats will expand gradually and indefinitely. Cottage pink will self-sow, but is seldom invasive. Under favorable conditions, it is hardy and long-lived.

How to start: Divisions or nursery plants are most frequently used. It is also easily grown from cuttings in the spring. The plant is easy to start from seed, but this will result in considerable variation.

Where to plant: Sharply drained soil, preferably on the alkaline side. It performs best in sandy soil amended with organic matter to retain moisture during the dry seasons. Give it full sun and good air circulation. Most cottage pinks are not for southern climates with hot, muggy summers, and do best in cool coastal or mountainous areas of northern latitudes. Space plants 12 to 15 inches apart. Hardy to zone 3.

Care: Moderately easy. Water during drought. Shear the flowers toward the end of the blooming season to encourage new growth and prevent reseeding. Leaf spot may become a problem in muggy weather or in crowded conditions. Apply a fungicide as soon as it is detected. Division is best performed in early spring, and is one of the best means of increase. It also may be necessary every third or fourth year to prevent overcrowding.

Related species and varieties: *Dianthus* × *Allwoodii* is a hybrid strain generally agreed to be derived from crosses between the carnation and the cottage pink. The foliage is a bit more coarse and the plant stockier than *D. plumarius*, growing to about 12 inches tall. It is reportedly more tolerant of the hot, muggy summers of the Southeast.

D. caryophyllus (Carnation) includes types sold as annuals; but, although they are among the most tender of the species, all are true perennials. The

hardiest border carnations will often survive temperatures as low as 12° if protected by evergreen boughs. They are quite fragrant, much more so than greenhouse carnations.

D. deltoides (Maiden Pink) is a low-growing, mat-forming species with small, profuse flowers in June. The turflike foliage is semievergreen, often turning blackish and persisting throughout the winter.

Dicentra spectabilis
(Bleeding Heart)
Dutchman's Breeches family. Native to Japan.

The flowers of the bleeding heart are aptly named. They are puffy and suggest a heart with two "drops of blood" flaring up and out from the base, resulting in an overall lyre shape. The blossoms are rose-pink with white tips, pink, or occasionally white in color, and hang pendulously from horizontally arching and drooping stems. The racemes are up to 9 inches long, and are produced among and on top of the foliage.

The foliage is medium green, often with a slightly grayish cast, with deeply cut leaves that give the plant a finely textured appearance. The plant forms dense clumps of arching sprays of foliage 30 inches tall and up to 36 inches wide. Because of its relatively large size and a tendency to die down after blooming, it is best used as a specimen rather than massed, and used with accompanying plants that will succeed its effect later in the season. It is an especially excellent specimen plant in partial shade.

How to start: Young plants purchased from a nursery are best planted in the spring before the new growth

starts. Bleeding heart can be started from seed, but this requires patience. Sow seed outdoors in late fall or early winter, or start indoors by sowing them in small flats, freezing them for 6 weeks, then taking them out and germinating at 55° to 60°. Seedlings should appear in 3 to 5 weeks.

Where to plant: The plant prefers rich, moist, well-drained soil high in organic matter; and partial shade. It will tolerate full sun or deep shade quite well; however, in full sun the foliage can be expected to burn and die back quickly after flowering. It is also best to keep the plant out of drying winds. Space plants 2 feet apart if not growing as a single specimen. Hardy to zone 2.

Care: Easy to moderately easy. Water abundantly and feed regularly, but cut back when the dormant period begins. Cultivars advertised as "blooming all summer" require the regular removal of spent blossoms. The chief problem is stem rot, which results from soggy soil and poor drainage. It is best not to disturb this plant; division is seldom successful, and not necessary.

Related species and varieties: *Dicentra eximia* (Fringed Bleeding Heart) is notable for its beautiful gray-green, finely dissected foliage, which contrasts effectively with its deep rose-to-white flowers. It also has a longer bloom season. Several hybrid forms of this plant (probably crosses with *D. formosa*, among others) will bloom intermittently all summer long if faded blossoms are removed regularly. One example is the beautiful hybrid 'Bountiful', with intense, deep red flowers off and on from June until frost.

D. formosa (Western Bleeding Heart) is an aggressive spreader with flower stems about 1 foot tall and blossoms rose-purple to white in color.

Dictamnus albus

Digitalis purpurea
'Excelsior' hybrids

Dictamnus albus
(Gas Plant)
Citrus family. Native from southern
Europe to northern China.

The gas plant is a large, bushy perennial with showy flowers in early summer and excellent, clean, long-lasting
foliage useful for background. A lit
match held just below a blossom will ig-
nite the minute amount of gas it re-
leases with a soft "pop," and no injury
to the flower.

The flowers are white, pink, or purplish. Individually they are irregular
and small, about 1 inch across, but are
produced in great quantities in spikes
at the top of the plant. They bloom in
late May and June.

The foliage is medium green, dense,
and of medium texture, and remains
attractive until frost. When the leaves
are brushed or crushed, they exude the
fragrance of lemons, to which the plant
is related.

Gas plant forms dense clumps of vertical and slightly arching stems with
many lateral branches. It grows to 3
feet high, and with age often spreads
twice as wide, the clumps gradually en-
larging by expanding rhizomes. It is
quite long-lived

How to start: Setting out young
nursery plants is by far the most common method. This should be done in
spring. To start from seed, sow outdoors in late fall or early winter. They
will germinate the following spring, but
it is best to wait another year to transplant them. Seedlings do not take well
to transplanting, so it is better to plant
in individual pots.

Where to plant: The plant prefers
rich, well-drained soil high in organic
matter. Avoid wet, soggy soils. Give it
full sun or light shade. Allow 3 feet on
all sides. Hardy to zone 2.

Care: Easy. Gas plant responds to occasional feeding during the growing
season. It has no serious pests. Division
is never necessary and if tried is seldom
successful. It resents transplanting and
disturbance.

Related species and varieties: Dictamnus albus, the species, has pure white
flowers.

D. albus var. purpureus has deep pink
or rosy-purple flowers.

Digitalis purpurea
(Foxglove)
Snapdragon family. Native to the
western Mediterranean region.

While a true biennial, the foxglove self-
sows generously, and is thus usually
considered a permanent fixture in the
garden. The tall spikes of colorful
flowers atop leafy stems lend an outstanding vertical effect, most valuable at
the rear of the border. The plant is
also excellent for informal, naturalistic
plantings.

Flowers come in purple, pink, white,
reddish, or yellow, often with a spotted
throat. Individually they are tubular,
about 2½ inches long, inclined at a
downward tilt, and are produced along
one side of tall, erect stems. Each ra-
ceme of flowers, often 1 or 2 feet long,
starts blooming at the base and ends
at the top. They appear in June and
July.

How the plant arrived at its common
name is open to question. Apart from
the common notion that it refers to

gloves for a fox, some contend that the
word is derived from "folks' gloves," re-
ferring to gloves wearable by fairies
("folks"). Others believe that it is a cor-
ruption of "folks' glauve," which in me-
dieval English meant a hand-held set
of bells (glauve) of a size appropriate to
fairies. Others judiciously skirt the
issue.

The leaves are large, somewhat
rough and wrinkled, and dark green on
the upper surface and light green be-
neath, where they are covered with
whitish hairs. They are dense at the
base of the plant, becoming smaller and
more scarce toward the top.

Foxglove grows 2 to 5 feet tall. It is
biennial, and will sometimes bloom a
second time with smaller spikes if the
flowers are removed before they can set
seed. The plant self-sows abundantly,
but cannot be relied upon to do so unless conditions are favorable. The foliage tends to look unattractive after
blooming is complete.

How to start: Plant nursery plants in
spring. Or sow outdoors in late spring
or early summer, or indoors at a constant temperature of 70°. Do not cover
the seeds. Germination occurs in 1 to
3 weeks.

Where to plant: Acid, moist, well-
drained soil high in organic matter.
The plant is partial to deep shade, but
tolerates full sun. Hybrid varieties are
usually less particular about soil. Space
plants 18 to 24 inches apart. Hardy to
zone 4.

Care: Moderately easy. Removing
flower spikes before they set seed will
encourage second-year bloom, but it
will be inferior. Otherwise allow the
plants to self-sow and remove unattractive plants after their seed is dispersed.
Regular applications of fungicide to

Doronicum cordatum

Echinacea purpurea
'Bright Star'

protect from powdery mildew and leaf spot, and of insecticide to protect from aphids, mealybugs, and Japanese beetles, may prove beneficial. Division is not applicable, as the plants usually die after they flower.

Related species and varieties: The Excelsior Hybrids are the best choice, because they produce flowers on all sides of the stem. The flowers are so tightly packed that they do not droop, as does the species, but are held at right angles to the stem. They come in pastel shades of pink, white, yellow, and rose, usually in mixes.

There are some truly perennial species of foxglove, but they have fewer and less colorful flowers.

Doronicum cordatum
(Leopard's Bane)
Daisy family. Native to southeastern Europe and western Asia.

The spring-blooming, daisylike, bright yellow flowers of leopard's bane appear in great quantities above clusters of large, heart-shape leaves.

Each blossom is 2 to 3 inches across and appears on its own 9- to 15-inch stem. The plant blooms in May, and the foliage declines and often dies down after blooming is complete.

The foliage is of medium to coarse texture and is produced in low basal clumps of 3- to 5-inch leaves medium to bright green in color. The clumps grow 8 to 12 inches high, and with flowers the plant often reaches 2 to 3 feet in height, spreading nearly as wide.

Leopard's bane produces shallow, dense, fibrous roots. The clumps expand rapidly and start dying out in the center unless divided. Since the foliage dies out early in the season, the plant is best used as a specimen rather than massed, and should be combined with other plants that will succeed the empty space. In warm climates with mild, long autumns, the foliage may come back and the plant bloom again.

How to start: Nursery plants or divisions, taken in August while the plant is dormant. Or sow seed outdoors in late spring or summer. Germination is slow and erratic, but usually occurs within 4 weeks.

Where to plant: Rich, moist soil high in organic matter. It prefers partial shade, especially in hot climates. Space plants 12 to 15 inches apart. Hardy to zone 4.

Care: Easy. Water moderately during the growing season. There are no serious pests. Division for rejuvenation is usually required every 2 to 4 years, and is best done during dormancy in August or very early spring. It is an excellent means of increase.

Echinacea purpurea
(Purple Coneflower)
Daisy family. Native from Ohio to Iowa, south to Louisiana and Georgia.

The purple coneflower is a large, coarse plant with daisylike flowers that have relaxed, drooping "petals." Named varieties are much superior to the species.

The flowers come in purple and, occasionally, white varieties. The "petals," technically ray flowers, droop back toward the stem. The eye is conical, bristly, and colored with purple, maroon, or brown. The flowers are 3 to 4 inches wide and appear at the ends of many long, branched stems. They bloom in July to September.

The foliage is dull green and composed of large, coarse-textured leaves that are dense at the base of the plant, smaller and more scattered toward the top. The plant forms a clump of many stems, which are branched, semi-erect, and spreading.

Purple coneflower grows 3 to 5 feet high and 2 to 5 feet wide. It is long-lived and not invasive.

How to start: Divisions or started root cuttings from a nursery. Seeds will not produce plants true to type, but will result in many inferior plants.

Where to plant: Soil should be sandy and well drained. Provide full sun or light shade; the latter produces richer colors. The plant is native to North American prairies and meadows, mostly at the edges of woods. It is drought and wind tolerant. Space plants 18 to 24 inches apart. Hardy to zone 3.

Care: Moderately easy. It responds to light feeding and moderate watering. Never allow the soil to remain soggy. Japanese beetles can ruin this plant very quickly; protect it with traps or insecticide. Clumps will require division every third or fourth year for rejuvenation. This is also an excellent means of increase, and should be performed in early spring just as new growth appears.

Varieties: It is best to purchase named varieties, as most have bigger flowers and better color than the species.

'The King' is probably the most famous hybrid. Its 6-inch flowers are a brilliant reddish purple with brown centers. It grows to 3 feet and has a more refined appearance.

'White Lustre' has creamy white flowers that are produced in incredible profusion, even in severe drought. Its foliage and structure, however, are quite coarse.

Euphorbia epithymoides

Echinops exaltatus 'Veitch's Blue'
Echinops exaltatus 'Blue Globe'

Echinops exaltatus
(Globe Thistle)
Daisy family. Native to Russia.

Globe thistles are large, bold plants with round flower heads and spiny, toothed leaves.

The flowers, which bloom in July through August, are various shades of blue. Individually tiny, they are gathered into dense, bristly balls about 2 inches across. These balls occur singly at the ends of branched stems, and dry well for winter flower arrangements.

The leaves are deep green on the upper surface and white on the lower. Deeply toothed, they present a coarse appearance. The plant produces dense clumps of semi-erect, spreading stems. The clumps expand gradually and require periodic thinning. However, the roots are dense and about 1 foot deep, and thus difficult to divide. The plants tend to lose leaves at the base as the season progresses.

How to start: Divisions or young container plants from a nursery are best. Always be sure to acquire named varieties. Plant in early spring. Seedlings are extremely variable and usually inferior.

Where to plant: Well-drained soil of only average fertility. Rich soil will produce taller, more open plants. Full sun is best, but the plant tolerates partial shade. It withstands considerable drought, but responds to adequate moisture. It is utterly intolerant of soggy soil. Space plants 18 to 24 inches apart. Hardy to zone 3.

Care: Moderately easy. Globe thistle requires little special attention and has no serious pests. Although difficult due to the deep and extensive root system, division is necessary every third or fourth year. It is an excellent means of increase, and is best done in early spring.

Varieties: The best cultivar is 'Taplow Blue', which has steel-blue, 3-inch flower heads.

Euphorbia epithymoides
formerly *E. polychroma*
(Cushion Spurge)
Spurge family. Native to eastern Europe.

The bright yellow-green floral bracts in spring, an excellent, neat, mounded habit, and clean foliage all summer long make this plant attractive as a specimen or at the front of the border.

The true flowers are minute and yellow, but each is surrounded by large, leafy, bright chartreuse bracts. Bloom appears in late April to early June.

The dark green leaves, covered with whitish hairs, turn a rich dark red in fall. Of medium texture, the foliage is pest-free and attractive all season. The plant is thick with leaves held tightly against the stems, forming a dense mound 1 to 2 feet high.

The plant is more restrained in growth and less invasive than some other spurges; however, it will self-sow. Cushion spurge is long-lived.

How to start: Young nursery plants should be set out in early spring. It is also easy to start from seed sown outdoors in late fall or early spring.

Where to plant: The plant tolerates nearly any soil, but can spread invasively if soil is rich and moist. It will take dry, poor soils and remain in excellent condition. Give it full sun. The neat, symmetrical habit is best as a specimen, but if planted in groups, space them 12 to 15 inches apart. Hardy to zone 4.

Care: Easy. Spurges are quite tolerant of drought, heat, and neglect. There are no serious pests. It resents disturbance and does not transplant well. In rich, moist soil, careful division in either spring or fall may be necessary to check excessive spreading.

Related species: *Euphorbia corollata* (Flowering Spurge) is quite unlike cushion spurge. It produces misty sprays of tiny white flowers, resembling baby's breath, in July and August; and the foliage turns a deep red in fall. It self-sows plentifully, is extremely tough and adaptable, and never needs staking.

E. cyparissus (Cyprus Spurge) is low, bushy, and mat-forming. It has narrow, linear leaves of fine texture, and yellow-green floral bracts in May and June. It is best planted in dry, poor soil, such as in a stony bank, as it will become a rampant weed in soil of even average fertility and moisture.

E. myrsinites (Myrtle Euphorbia) is evergreen and very hardy. The gray-green foliage is produced on trailing, fleshy stems only 3 to 6 inches high and over a foot long. It tends to spread invasively by creeping, rooting stems, and by massive seed production. It can be excellent, however, trailing down a rock wall or as a ground cover in dry, poor soil. It is the most highly recommended spurge for the Deep South.

Filipendula rubra

Gaillardia × grandiflora 'Goblin'

Filipendula rubra
(Queen of the Prairie)
Rose family. Native from Pennsylvania to Iowa, and south to Georgia and Kentucky.

This is a tall, stately plant with large, feathery pink plumes in midsummer and lush foliage that remains attractive all season. It is a fine choice for the rear of the border.

The individual flowers are tiny, but together form plumes at the ends of the stems. The effect is delicate and finely textured. Flowers appear in late June through July.

The medium green, compound leaves are dense and lush. The plant produces clumps of numerous erect, leafy stems 4 to 6 feet high, each bearing flowers at the top. The clumps expand gradually by slowly creeping rhizomes. It is restrained in growth, never invasive, and long-lived.

How to start: Nursery plants or divisions made in spring. If started by seed, it must be fresh and should be sown outdoors in early fall.

Where to plant: As native habitat is the moist, deep soil of bottomland prairies and meadows, plant the queen of the prairie in fertile, moist soil high in organic matter. It flowers best in full sun, but is quite tolerant of partial shade. Space plants 12 to 24 inches apart. Hardy to zone 3.

Care: Moderately easy. Water abundantly and feed regularly. During wet or humid weather mildew may present a problem. Control with fungicide. While the plant seldom requires division for rejuvenation, it is an excellent means of increase. Divide in early spring just as the new growth begins.

Related species and varieties: *Filipendula hexapetala* (Dropwort) grows only to 2 feet. Misty clusters of ivory flowers, single or double, appear in June and are held above finely textured, ferny foliage. It withstands drought and poor soil better than other filipendulas, and is the best choice for the Southeast, where the foliage frequently is evergreen. The double 'Flore Pleno' hybrid flowers longer than the species.

F. rubra var. *venusta* (Martha Washington Plume) is superior to the species, with huge, 12-inch, feathery plumes that are deep, bright pink. It blooms in July and early August.

F. ulmaria (Queen of the Meadow) is similar to *F. rubra*, except that the flowers are white. Growing to 4 feet, it blooms in June to mid-July.

Gaillardia × grandiflora
(Blanket Flower)
Daisy family. Of hybrid origin, parents native to the mountainous West and the Southeast in the United States.

The blanket flower is a relatively short-lived perennial with bright red, bronze, or yellow flowers, often in combination. Best planted in the front of the border in groups of three or more, it provides bloom all summer long.

The daisylike flowers have outer rays that can be solid or bicolored, and a central eye that can be yellow, brown, or purple. They are 3 to 4 inches across, and appear at the ends of leafy stems in great quantities, blooming in June to September.

The foliage is dark green, dense, and of medium texture, with hairy, lance-shape leaves. Gaillardia forms clumps of multibranched, erect to spreading stems, and can grow to 3 feet tall. The plant spreads outward by underground rhizomes. It is usually quite short-lived.

How to start: Easiest by nursery plants or divisions made in early spring. Named varieties purchased as young plants from the nursery are usually root cuttings. Plants usually do not come true from seed, but to start by seed, sow outdoors in early spring or summer for flowering plants the next season. Or sow indoors in late winter at a constant 70°. Do not cover seed, as it requires light to germinate.

Where to plant: Soil must be very well drained and of average to poor fertility. Rich, moist soils, especially if wet over winter, lead to an open, sprawling habit and an early death. Give it full sun. It tolerates heat and drought well. Space plants 10 to 15 inches apart. Hardy to zone 2.

Care: Do not overwater or overfertilize. Remove spent flowers before they set seed to prolong the bloom period. Taller plants may require staking.

A regular program of both insecticide and fungicide will help prevent leaf spot, powdery mildew, aster yellows, and damage from various sucking insects. Carefully remove and destroy any plant infected with aster yellows.

Blanket flower requires annual division to perpetuate blooming from year to year. During the summer, prune roots by inserting a spade in a circle 6 inches around the crown. This stimulates the production of new plants from the severed roots. Transplant these in early spring. This process should be performed annually, as the plants are short-lived.

Geum coccineum 'Red Wings'

Geranium himalayense

Geranium sanguineum
(Bloodred Geranium)
Geranium family. Native to Eurasia.

The bloodred geranium (named for its fall foliage color) is a hardy herbaceous perennial with deeply cut leaves, a mounded, spreading form, and small, single magenta flowers. It should not be confused with the tender perennial or annual *Pelargonium*, which is often called geranium in the trade.

Flower varieties come in purplish-pink, red, or white. The blossoms are from 1 to 2 inches wide, have five petals, and appear at the ends of stems rising to 8 inches above the foliage. They bloom in May to August.

The bright green leaves have five lobes, are medium to fine in texture, and turn a bright red in the fall. They are produced densely. The plant forms mounds up to 2 feet wide, 1½ feet tall. It is long-lived, and may spread and self-sow invasively.

How to start: Sow fresh seed outdoors in early spring, or indoors at a constant 70°. Germination should occur in 1 to 5 weeks. Starting by divisions made in spring, or stem cuttings made in summer, can be equally successful.

Where to plant: Geraniums adapt to most soils, except wet or very dry ones, and are best with good drainage. Give them either full sun or partial shade. Soils of only average fertility are best, as rich, moist soils promote invasive growth. Space plants 12 inches apart. Hardy to zone 3.

Care: Moderately easy. Do not over-fertilize. The plant is little disturbed by pests, but the four-lined plant bug has been reported a problem. Bloodred geranium will require rejuvenation by division every 3 or 4 years. This is also an excellent means of increase, and should be done in spring.

Related species and varieties: *Geranium endressii* grows 15 to 18 inches high, and is best known for its varieties 'Johnson's Blue', with light gentian-blue flowers; and 'Wargrave Pink', with clear pink flowers. Both plants will flower over a long season, nearly all summer, if cut back after the first wave of blooms in May.

G. himalayense (Lilac Cranesbill), formerly *G. grandiflorum*, has blue, purple, or lavender flowers during May and July on 2-foot, mounded, spreading plants.

G. sanguineum var. *prostratum* (often erroneously called *G. lancastriense*) is more restrained and neat in growth habit than the species, seldom taller than 6 or 8 inches, with bright rose-pink blossoms nearly all summer long.

Geum
hybrids
(Geum; Avens)
Rose family. The various parents are native to the colder temperate regions in both the northern and southern hemispheres.

The many hybrid varieties of geum produce long, branching stems bearing flowers in bright reds, oranges, and yellows, often in electric hues. They are attractive both as specimens and in the mixed border.

The flowers are small, up to about 1 inch across, and single, with double and semidouble varieties. They appear in great profusion in May to August, and even longer if spent flowers are removed before they can set seed.

The stems and flowers radiate in all directions from dense basal clumps of large, deep-green leaves. Irregular and toothed, the leaves also appear on the 24- to 30-inch stems, becoming smaller and fewer as they ascend. The stems are multibranched and open.

While all avens grow slowly, the newer hybrids are even slower to increase; however, they are also longer-lived. The plants are never invasive.

How to start: The best results come with named varieties from nursery plants or divisions made in late summer. The latter will usually bloom the next spring. They are also easily started from seed sown outdoors in spring or summer, but the hybrids will not breed true, and considerable variation will result. Germination is of low percentage, so sow thickly.

Where to plant: The plant is quite choosy about location. The soil must have excellent drainage and a reasonable amount of organic matter. Water abundantly during the growing season, but avoid wet soil in winter; it is fatal. Give them full sun. They are reliably hardy to very low temperatures if the soil is dry, and perform best in regions of cool summers. Space plants 12 to 18 inches apart. Hardy to zone 5.

Care: Moderately difficult unless planted correctly; otherwise, they need little attention. Remove spent flowers to keep plants neat and extend bloom into fall. Avens has no serious pests. Division is an excellent means of increase, and is best done in late summer. The older varieties will require division every other year, but the newer hybrids can often go for many years before needing rejuvenation.

Pennisetum alopecuroides, foreground, and *Calamagrostis epigeous,* rear

Deschampsia caespitosa

Grasses, ornamental

Andropogon scoparius (Little Bluestem). This native of the eastern United States is useful either for naturalizing or in the border. Growing from 1½ to 4 feet tall, it presents a stiffly upright form with finely textured, bluish-green leaves that turn bronze or reddish and remain attractive all winter. The fluffy, small white flowers and seeds are effective from July into winter. It will grow in nearly any soil, but prefers those that are well drained and dry. Give it full sun. A strikingly blue selection has recently become available, wholesaled out of Nebraska. Hardy to zone 4.

Arrhenatherum elatius var. **bulbosum** 'Variegatum' (Variegated Bulbous Oatgrass). This grass is loosely tufted and deciduous, with attractive, striped leaves that have a clean white margin. When in flower (June to September) the plants may reach 3 feet in height and spread. This cultivar may be invasive, especially in rich soils, but is still more restrained in growth than the species. It is easy to grow in rich soil and either full sun or partial shade. In hot weather the foliage may brown and turn unsightly; it is often recommended to cut this grass back once about midsummer. Divide every 2 to 3 years to maintain vigor. It is native to the grasslands of Europe and western Asia, and is hardy to zone 5.

Calamagrostis epigeous 'hortorum' (also listed as *Calamagrostis* × *acutiflora* 'Stricta') (Reed Grass). This cultivar of reed grass is considered indispensable by many advanced gardeners for its narrowly vertical habit from 3 to 6 feet tall. Rich, foxy, golden-red inflorescences that are attractive all winter long begin blooming in late June and July, which is quite early for most grasses. It is easy to grow in any fertile soil and full sun, as long as it is kept moist. Reed grass is one of the few grasses that will thrive in heavy, wet clay soil, and actually prefers boggy situations. Reed grass is native discontinuously from Northern Europe to East and South Africa. It is hardy to zone 5.

Cortaderia selloana (Pampas Grass). Perennial only in mild climates (zone 7 and south), this large, coarse grass is often of huge dimensions, from 4 to 20 feet high. It is upright and spreading to mounded in form, with huge, fluffy plumes of flowers up to 3 feet long atop stems that may reach 20 feet. The flowers can be whitish or buff in color, or a pale pink, and they appear in the fall (summer in the mildest climates). Pampas grass performs quite well in dry, poor soils, but fertile moist ones are best. It prefers full sun. Occasionally dwarf or pink selections are offered. A new selection with yellow-variegated leaves, 'Gold Band', has recently been introduced.

C. jubata is another species that is occasionally encountered in the trade, usually mistakenly identified as *C. selloana*. *C. jubata* self-sows profusely and likely will become a noxious pest, especially in the milder climates of the West Coast. Unfortunately, it is extremely difficult to differentiate from pampas grass, especially when immature.

Deschampsia caespitosa (Tufted Hair Grass). Forming a 3-foot, finely textured, tufted mound, this hair grass is useful either in sun or shade, in moist soil or dry. The leaves are evergreen and effective all winter long. Feathery, whitish green flowers are produced from late June through August, which is early for most grasses. Hardy to zone 5.

Cortaderia selloana

Elymus arenarius,
with *Lychnis flos-jovis* in foreground

Festuca ovina 'Glauca'

Festuca ovina 'Glauca'

Hakonechloa macra 'Aureo-variegata'

Elymus arenarius (Blue Lyme Grass). Silvery blue foliage is the distinctive feature of this coarse, invasive grass. Unless it is restrained, the persistent, creeping rhizomes can become quite a nuisance. It grows 2 to 4 feet tall and the leaves tend to grow in every direction, creating a jumbled, coarse appearance. Blue lyme grass will grow in nearly any soil, but is intolerant of shade. Hardy to zone 4.

Festuca ovina 'Glauca' (Dwarf Blue Fescue). This is a popular, small, tufted grass with finely textured, silvery blue evergreen foliage. It grows from 6 to 12 inches high in a neat mound. It must have well-drained soil, and prefers full sun or light shade. Frequent division is required as the center of the clump will die out, especially in moist, rich soil. Removing the flowers as they appear tends to prolong its useful life. In Southern California, festuca is one of the few gray plants that will do well with light shade. Its color is better without the browning at the tips sometimes caused by the sun. Hardy to zone 4.

Hakonechloa macra 'Aureo-variegata' This grass is a relatively recent introduction to U.S. horticulture from the mountains and forests of Japan. The long, deciduous, arching leaves are variegated creamy yellow.   The plant spreads slowly by rhizomes, and is never invasive. Equally effective in pots or planted in large drifts, the plant presents a neat, uniform appearance, reaching up to 12 inches high. Grow this grass in acid (pH 5.5 to 6.0) soil that has both excellent drainage and plenty of organic matter. Bright indirect light is best. Full sun is not recommended. The plant is hardy to at least zone 4.

Helictotrichon sempervirens, formerly *Avena sempervirens* (Blue Oat Grass). Resembling a large blue fescue, this tufted, mounded grass with bluish-green leaves reaches 2 to 3 feet high. The leaves are of fine texture. Plant it in any soil in full sun. In humid environments it is prone to fungal attack. The foliage browns slightly in winter. Hardy to zone 5.

Miscanthus sinensis (Eulalia Grass). Large, striking, upright and gracefully arching at the top, *Miscanthus* forms dense clumps 6 to 12 feet tall. The foliage is medium-fine in texture, turning a rich gold that is effective through the winter. The flowers, with their pinkish or silvery 7- to 10-inch plumes, are also attractive from fall into winter. The plant will perform well in any soil, and should have full sun. Hardy to zone 4.

'Gracillimus' is a finely textured cultivar with narrow, somewhat curly leaves. 'Variegatus' and 'Zebrinus' have foliage and stems in combinations of green with yellow or white. These cultivars are smaller than the species, rarely exceeding 6 or 7 feet in height.

Molinia caerulea 'Variegata' (Purple Moor Grass). This is a densely tufted, deciduous grass hardy to zone 5. The leaves are medium to fine in texture and longitudinally striped with creamy white. The flowers are purplish pink, up to 16 inches long, and appear in late summer and early fall. The plant ranges from 18 to 24 inches high and wide. This grass prefers acid to neutral soil, and full sun. It dislikes alkaline soil. It is native to open moorlands and heaths of Europe and Southwest and northern Asia.

Helictotrichon sempervirens

Elymus arenarius (left),
Miscanthus sinensis 'Gracillimus' (center),
and Staghorn Sumac, right

Pennisetum alopecuroides (Fountain Grass). One of the most graceful and popular of ornamental perennial grasses, fountain grass grows in a loose tuft 2 to 3½ feet high. From late August through October, coppery-tan flowers arch out from the mound like water spraying out of a fountain. In late fall the flowers shatter and the foliage turns yellow. Give it full sun and a fertile soil, and enough room to develop its 3- to 4-foot mature diameter. It is native to open ground and steppes of Asia, and is hardy to zone 5.

Gypsophila paniculata
species and hybrids
(Baby's Breath)
Pink family. Native from central and eastern Europe to central Africa.

Gypsophila's cloudlike mists of tiny white or pink flowers are a familiar sight in the perennial garden. Use them as a complement to bold-textured plants, or as a focal point in the border.

The flowers are usually white, but some varieties are pink or have a pinkish cast. The individual blossoms are tiny, either single or double, and are produced in massive quantities on slender, multibranched stems. The effect is airy and delicate. They bloom in July, but this can be prolonged into September by shearing spent flowers.

The smooth, grayish green leaves are rarely noticeable below the drifts of flowers. The many stems are covered to the ground with blossoms, making the overall shape rounded and fluffy. Baby's breath reaches 3 feet high and as wide, often even wider. The plant is long-lived in a favorable location, and is never invasive. It forms thick, dense, fleshy roots.

How to start: Easy from seed sown outdoors in spring or early summer, if the species is desired. Or sow indoors in spring at 60° to 70°. Named cultivars, often superior, are generally grafted onto the species rootstock. These should be purchased and planted in early spring. Be sure to set the grafted varieties with the graft union 1 inch below the soil level.

Where to plant: The soil must be well drained and alkaline, and preferably low in fertility. Soggy soil, especially in winter, is usually fatal. Rock garden conditions are ideal. Give it full sun. Space plants 24 to 30 inches apart. Hardy to zone 3.

Care: Moderately easy. The plant is difficult to stake, and large varieties and vigorous plants will need support to keep from flopping and spreading open. The best method is to place a wire basket about 15 to 18 inches high and wide over young plants for the stems to grow through. In acid soils apply lime yearly, but do not let it come into direct contact with the fleshy roots. To prolong bloom, keep flowers sheared before they set seed. Once established, it needs little attention.

Although the plant is usually free of pests and disease, leaf hoppers and aster yellows have been reported. North of zone 6, mulching over the winter to protect from cold is advised; however, do not cover the crown until after the ground is completely frozen, or rotting is likely.

The thick, fleshy roots are difficult to divide, and plants resent the disturbance of transplanting. Division is discouraged, but if undertaken should be done in spring.

Gypsophila paniculata

Related species and varieties: 'Bristol Fairy' is the most common cultivar, with excellent double white flowers on 4-foot plants.

'Pink Fairy' is a small, restrained plant growing only 18 inches high. It has a long bloom season, producing pink double flowers from July to frost.

Gypsophila repens is a low-growing species from 6 to 18 inches high that spreads widely by creeping, rooting stems. It is good in the front of the border, in the rock garden, or trailing down walls. One of the most popular varieties is a pink form, 'Rosy Veil'.

Helianthus 'Italian White'

Helenium 'Sunny Boy'

Heliopsis helianthoides
subspecies *scabra*

Helenium autumnale
(Sneezeweed)
Daisy family. Native to most of
continental North America.

Sneezeweed is an unfortunate name for
this plant, as it neither causes sneezing
nor is it a weed. The small, daisylike
flowers, despite their massive quantity,
present a delicate appearance in the
garden, as the rays of each flower head
point gracefully back toward the stem.
It is a relative of the sunflower and the
black-eyed Susan.

Flowers occur in shades of red, orange, or yellow, with solid or bicolored
"petals," or rays. The flowers are 1 or 2
inches across and appear at the ends
of branched stems. They bloom in late
July through frost.

The medium to dark green leaves
are linear, up to 6 inches long, and
larger and more numerous at the base
of the plant. The stems are erect, then
arch and spread at the top, making the
plant wider at the top than at the base.
Helenium can grow from 30 inches to 6
feet tall, depending upon variety and
growing conditions.

These are vigorous plants and will
rapidly overcrown if not divided regularly. Grown properly, they are long-
lived and seldom invasive.

How to start: The cultivars, which
are usually hybrid, will not breed true
from seed. But the species can be sown
indoors in early spring at 60° to germinate in 1 week. Purchased plants are
usually grown from stem cuttings or divisions, and are best planted in early
spring.

Where to plant: Best in soil of only
average fertility that is high in moisture
and organic matter. They are tolerant
of many poor soils, however, including
heavy, wet clay. Give them full sun.
Space plants 18 to 24 inches apart.
Hardy to zone 3.

Care: Moderately easy. The taller varieties need staking. Pinch growing tips
regularly until mid-June to promote
heavier flowering and bushy, dense
growth. Sneezeweeds have few serious
problems, although rust and leaf spot
have been reported. Division should be
performed every other year to prevent
overcrowding. Vigorous plants may
need annual division, but slower-grow-
ing hybrids may go as long as 4 years
without it.

Helianthus decapetalus
var. *multiflorus*
(Thinleaf Sunflower)
Daisy family. Native from Maine to
Georgia, and west to Illinois and
Minnesota.

This large, bushy sunflower produces
great quantities of yellow or gold
flowers in late summer. The blooms resemble dahlias, and are excellent in the
border and for cut flowers.

The blossoms may be either single or
double and are 3 to 4 inches in diameter. They appear in clusters at the ends
of branched stems, blooming from August until frost.

Unlike many other sunflowers, the
foliage usually stays attractive all season
long. The large, oval leaves are a dark,
dull green. The leafy stems are erect
and somewhat spreading toward the
top, where they become increasingly
branched. Most varieties reach 4 to 5
feet high.

The plant forms swollen, fleshy roots
similar to tubers. It is long-lived, restrained in growth, and never invasive.

How to start: It is best to purchase
named cultivars from the nursery, or to
divide selected plants in spring, as seed
results in many inferior plants.

Where to plant: These sunflowers
are native to moist woods and bottom
meadows, and so prefer moist, well-
drained soil high in organic matter. Although full sun is best, partial shade is
tolerated well. Good air circulation is
a distinct advantage. Space plants 18 to
24 inches apart. Hardy to zone 3.

Care: Easy. The tallest varieties may
require staking. Water adequately and
feed occasionally. It has few serious
pests, although mildew can be a problem in moist locations with poor air circulation. Protect plants with fungicide.
Division is the best means of increase,
but is seldom needed for rejuvenation.
Divide in early spring.

Heliopsis helianthoides
subspecies *scabra*
(Heliopsis)
Daisy family. Native to eastern North
America.

The yellow or gold flowers of heliopsis
are produced in incredible abundance
over a long season. For its bright, solid
color and length of bloom, it is nearly
indispensable in the mixed border.

The flowers may be single or semidouble, but most cultivars are fully
double. Resembling zinnias, they are
3 to 4 inches across and appear at the
ends of long, branched, leafy stems.
They bloom from early July to frost.

Helleborus niger
Hemerocallis 'Just Mary'
Hemerocallis 'George Cunningham'

The dark green leaves are lush, dense, and lance-shape or oblong to 5 inches in length. The plant is erect to spreading, bushy, and widest at the top. It grows 3 to 4 feet high. Always restrained in growth and never invasive, it is long-lived when divided periodically.

How to start: Best to divide named cultivars in fall or spring, or to plant nursery plants. Plants may vary considerably when started from seed.

Where to plant: Best in moist, well-drained soil of average to moderately high fertility and high in organic matter. Give it full sun. Space plants 24 inches apart. Hardy to zone 3.

Care: Moderately easy. Water abundantly, especially during drought. Fertilize regularly. Aphids are the chief pest problem, especially on plants grown in poor soil. Otherwise, there are no serious pests. Rejuvenate by dividing every 3 or 4 years. Division is also the best means of increase.

Helleborus niger
(Christmas Rose)
Buttercup family. Native to Europe.

Not even remotely related to roses, this is an evergreen perennial that blooms in winter with large white flowers, often flushed with pale pink. It is useful in shady woodland spots under the canopy of deciduous trees.

The flowers are produced at the ends of several clustered stems. They have five showy sepals, 2 to 4 inches across, surrounding a center of attractive yellow stamens. They can bloom as early as November or as late as March or April, although the latter is more common. Winter bloom depends upon warm spells that thaw the soil.

The foliage appears to grow directly out of the soil without stems. The large, smooth, deep green leaves are compound, divided into seven or more leaflets, and are evergreen in zone 6 and south.

The clumps of foliage expand slowly by rhizomatous roots. The plant grows to 15 inches high and is long-lived, restrained in growth, and never invasive.

How to start: Best started from nursery plants or divisions planted in spring. It can be started from seed, but this takes considerable time to result in plants large enough to transplant. Young (first-year) self-sown seedlings collected from around established plants are easy to transplant.

Where to plant: Well-drained, moist soil high in organic matter and preferably acid or neutral (pH 6.5 to 7.0). The plant requires shade in summer and partial sun in winter, such as is found under the boughs of deciduous trees or shrubs (but try to avoid competing, greedy roots). Hardy to zone 3.

Care: Moderately difficult, being choosy about location. Keep evenly moist and never allow it to dry out. Mulch well with organic matter in summer and irrigate regularly, especially during drought. If the soil is extremely acid, apply lime yearly, but avoid letting it contact the roots, which are sensitive. Fertilize rarely, if ever, as the roots are easily damaged by nitrogen.

Leaf spot is occasionally troublesome, but easy to treat with fungicide.

Christmas rose resents disturbance of any kind, and never needs division for rejuvenation. Dividing for increase is possible but difficult, and should be

performed in early spring after blooming is complete. Carefully separate the roots, ensuring that each portion has several roots and "eyes" (developing leaf buds). Set the roots so that the eyes are about an inch below soil level.

Related species and varieties: *Helleborus lividus* var. *corsicus* has apple-green blossoms in large clusters in early spring. This is the best helleborus for the mild-climate regions of the Southwest. Although reportedly hardy to zone 6, in the northern limits of its range it should be well protected from cold, drying winds in the winter.

H. orientalis (Lenten Rose) blooms from March into May. Varieties are available with flowers in colors from chocolate and purplish green to pink and white. The foliage is a lighter green than the Christmas rose, but the structure and cultural needs are nearly the same. It is hardy to zone 5 and is reported to be the best helleborus for the Southeast.

Hemerocallis
hybrids
(Daylily)
Lily family. Most hybrids have parents native to Japan.

Daylilies are very easy, long-lasting perennials with attractive foliage and showy flowers. The individual blossoms last only a day, but are continuously produced over a long season.

Daylilies come in many colors, with flowers in shades of cream, yellow, orange, red, pink, and violet; often striped and bicolored. Individually they are from 3 to 5 inches long, and open just as wide. They appear at the ends of long stems. Some varieties are deliciously fragrant.

Hemerocallis hybrids

Hemerocallis 'Northbrook Star'
Hemerocallis 'Finest Hour'

Flowering generally lasts 3 to 4 weeks, but this varies according to the cultivar. The bloom season is commonly divided into *early* (late May and June), *middle* (July), and *late* (August into September), although considerable overlapping occurs.

The bright green, handsome, straplike leaves grow 1 to 2 feet long, and are effective all season. The leaves arch out from the base of the plant, forming a mound of foliage. Stems and flowers arise from this mound.

Depending upon variety, daylilies can reach from 20 inches to 3 or 4 feet tall, including flowers. They all form a tough, heavy, tuberous root system. Some varieties are evergreen in mild climates (zone 8 and south).

Daylilies are exceedingly long-lived and clumps will expand indefinitely. They are restrained in growth, permanent, not invasive, and compete well with roots of trees and shrubs. Hybrids will not reseed.

How to start: Nursery stock or division in spring or late summer. Sowing seed is a complex and intriguing undertaking for those gardeners interested in selecting and breeding.

Where to plant: Daylilies are highly adaptable, but perform best in well-drained soil high in organic matter and of only average fertility. Tolerating shade or sun well, they seem to prefer full sun in northern areas, and partial shade in the hot South. However, delicate colors tend to fade quickly in full sun. Too rich a soil leads to the rapid growth of lush foliage and few flowers. Space plants 18 to 36 inches apart. Hardy to zone 3.

Care: Very easy. Water through dry periods and give an occasional light feeding. To improve appearance, remove the flower stalks after their blossoms are spent. The plant has no

serious pests. Although most varieties can be left alone permanently, some of the more vigorous ones give improved performance with division every 6 or 7 years. Division of mature plants is an arduous task due to the heavy root system, but it is still the best means of increase. Divide in spring or late summer.

Varieties: Cultivars are too numerous to mention here. Extensive breeding has resulted in thousands.

Heuchera sanguinea
and hybrids
(Coral Bells)
Saxifrage family. Native to New Mexico and Arizona, south to Mexico.

Airy clusters of tiny bell-shape flowers top the long, delicate flower stalks of coral bells. They are effective in the front of borders or as a small-scale ground cover in either sun or partial shade, and are hardy far north of their natural range.

The flowers are pink, red, white, or chartreuse. They bloom in June and July, but flowering can be prolonged into September by removing faded flower stalks.

The attractive basal clumps of foliage are evergreen. The leaves are dark or bright green, rounded, and 2 to 4 inches across. Some varieties are marbled with bronze or silver, and take on a reddish cast in fall that lasts through the winter. The plant grows 10 to 24 inches high.

The clumps of foliage will expand gradually from the center by the growth of long, fleshy surface roots. Although coral bells produces great quantities of seed, some of which may germinate in the garden, it could never be considered invasive. It is long-lived.

How to start: Nursery plants or division in spring are the most common methods of starting. Make sure that each thick stem has a few roots, and plant the crowns 1 inch below the soil level. Coral bells are also easy to start from leaf cuttings made in late fall. Each cutting needs a short section of leafstalk, in addition to an entire leaf, to root in sand. Seed sown outdoors in early spring will produce flowering plants the next year. Merely press the seed into the soil and do not cover, as it needs light to germinate. Or sow indoors in late winter or early spring at 50° to 60°. Germination takes about 20 days. Hybrid seed will not breed true.

Where to plant: Coral bells are quite adaptable, but perform best in well-drained soils rich in organic matter. They prefer full sun but do quite well in partial shade. Space plants 9 to 15 inches apart. Hardy to zone 3.

Care: Easy. Removing flower stalks before they can set seed and abundant watering over dry periods will prolong bloom. Owing to the shallow, fleshy roots, coral bells are prone to frost heave in winter; during warm spells and in spring, the crowns may have to be pushed back into the soil. A loose covering, such as evergreen boughs, may help alleviate this problem.

Root weevils and mealybugs can be problems, and protection with insecticide will help. Stem rot can be serious in heavy, wet soils and humid climates.

The plant probably will need rejuvenation by division every fifth or sixth year. When flowering is reduced and clumps have become woody, it is time to divide. Younger plants can be divided for increase, an excellent means of propagation that should be done in spring.

Heuchera sanguinea

Hibiscus moscheutos
'Southern Belle'

Hosta sieboldiana

Hibiscus moscheutos
(Rose Mallow)
Mallow family. Native to the marshes of the eastern United States.

Besides making an effective background to 8 feet tall and covered with large, bold leaves, the rose mallow produces huge, dramatic, plate-size flowers up to a foot across. Marginally hardy in northern regions, they are a most useful plant for gardens in the Southwest.

The flowers are red, pink, or white, often with contrasting blotches at the interior of the blossom. The blooms are single, 8 to 12 inches wide, and appear toward the tops of the branched stems. The bloom season is mid-July to frost. Flowering peaks in August, after which the blossoms decrease in size.

The leaves are green on the upper surface, whitish on the lower, oval, and up to 8 inches long. The foliage is dense.

The plant is erect to slightly spreading and from 5 to 8 feet high. Despite this height, the leafy stems are sturdy and rarely require staking. While they may self-sow freely in moist soil, rose mallows are generally restrained in growth and not invasive. They will live a long time.

How to start: Easy from seed. Soak the seeds in water until they drop to the bottom of the container, then sow outdoors in spring. Germination is very fast, usually within 3 or 4 days. The resulting plants usually will bloom the next year. Because there is considerable variation from seed, cultivars are best started from divisions in spring. Set the eyes (leaf buds) of the divisions 4 inches below soil level.

Where to plant: Rose mallows reach maximum size and lushness in wet, soggy soil high in organic matter; but they also perform well in average, well-drained garden soil. Give them either full sun or partial shade. Space them 24 to 30 inches apart. Hardy to zone 6, they are an excellent choice for the southern garden.

Care: Easy. Water abundantly in dry soils. Regular feeding will result in larger, lusher plants. Although Japanese beetles are attracted to the blossoms, the peak bloom season usually follows the peak beetle season. Leaf spot, canker, rust, blight, aphids, white fly, and scale can all be problems, although rarely serious. If necessary, protect the plants with a regular insecticide and fungicide program.

Division is never required for rejuvenation, but is the best means to increase a favorite cultivar. Divide either in spring or fall.

Hosta sieboldiana
(Blue-Leaf Plantain Lily)
Lily family. Native to Japan.

Lush, bold foliage is the outstanding feature of this plant. The large, bluish, heart-shape leaves fan out symmetrically from a central clump. It is an excellent choice for a bold statement in a problem shady spot.

The flowers are pale lilac to near white. They are like small lilies, 1½ inches long on short, erect stems, and occur in clusters of 6 to 10 blossoms. Often hidden by the foliage, they bloom in July.

The foliage is bright green when first emerging and assumes an effective powdery blue cast as the season progresses. The leaves are huge, 10 to 15 inches long and nearly as broad, and

somewhat wrinkled on the surface. They grow in a basal rosette, the clumps reaching 2½ feet high and up to 40 inches across. The bold texture of the foliage is effective all season long. White- and yellow-variegated cultivars are also available.

This long-lived plantain lily freely produces seed, which sometimes germinates, but it could never be called invasive. The variegated cultivars will not breed true from seed.

How to start: Plant nursery plants or divisions of young plants in spring. It can be grown successfully from seed, but sizable plants take 3 years or more to develop and will exhibit considerable variation.

Where to plant: Hosta tolerates a wide range of soils, but is best in well-drained, moist soil high in organic matter. Avoid wet, soggy soils. Either partial or deep shade is satisfactory. They normally flower less in deep shade, but with this species the flowers are nearly concealed anyway. Full sun is likely to burn the foliage. Space plants 30 to 36 inches apart. Hardy to zone 3.

Care: Easy. The plant needs little attention once established, but should be watered deeply and regularly during dry spells. Young plants may profit from a winter mulch, especially if planted in the fall.

Snails and slugs can be quite destructive; use bait for protection. Other chewing insects may also disfigure foliage. Crown rot can be a problem in wet winters if the soil is not well drained.

Hosta never requires division, and may last 30 years or more in the garden. To propagate, divide only young plants up to 3 years of age, as older plants develop a tough crown that is hard to separate and even more difficult to establish.

Hosta 'Chartreuse'

Iris 'Dazzling Gold'
(bearded hybrid)

Related species: Many species of hosta abound, ranging in leaf size from a diminutive 2 to 3 inches to the giant described above. Many have showy, sometimes fragrant flowers that add interest to the shady border, and some have variegated cultivars with white or yellow markings.

Hosta decorata (Blunt-Leaf Plantain Lily) produces 6-inch leaves rimmed with silvery white on compact, 2-foot plants. The flowers are a rich, dark violet, and are showy in August.

H. fortunei (Tall-Cluster Plantain Lily) produces many stems bearing showy clusters of small white or pale lavender flowers in August. The oval, light green leaves are 5 to 8 inches long. Several variegated cultivars are available.

H. lancifolia (Narrow-Leaf Plantain Lily) has slender, 6-inch dark green leaves. It produces great quantities of flower stalks bearing large clusters (up to thirty flowers each) of pale lilac flowers in August.

H. plantaginea (Fragrant Plantain Lily) is a popular old-time favorite with large, 4- to 5-inch fragrant white flowers produced in clusters from mid-August into September. The large, heart-shape leaves, up to 10 inches long, are light green and form a mound that can spread to 3 feet.

H. tardifolia (Autumn Plantain Lily) produces large clusters of deep purple flowers just above the leaves. It blooms very late in the season, in October. The plants are small, to 12 inches high and wide, with dainty, dark green narrow leaves 4 to 6 inches long.

H. undulata (Wavy-Leaf Plantain Lily) has both fascinating foliage and very showy flowers, with the added advantage of being more tolerant of full sun than any other hosta. The leaves have a wavy margin, are striped with white

and green, and are relatively small, 6 to 8 inches long. The pale violet flowers are generously produced on stems from 10 to 30 inches tall, and are quite showy in July.

H. ventricosa (Blue Plantain Lily) bears striking blue to deep violet flowers 2 inches long, generously arranged in clusters made up of ten to fifteen flowers. It blooms in July and August. The leaves grow up to 9 inches long and are oval with a delicate twist at the tip.

Iris
species and hybrids
(Bearded Iris)
Iris family. Most commonly grown varieties are of uncertain hybrid parentage, with parents native around the world, mostly in the north temperate zones.

Complex hybridization has resulted in a monumental number of iris cultivars to choose from. All have gray-green, swordlike leaves, and their large flowers are available in every color and color combination imaginable. Height ranges from dwarf bearded miniatures 4 to 6 inches tall to the stately, tall plants reaching 4 feet or more.

The three outer sepals of each flower are called "falls," and have a fuzzy central portion called a "beard." The three inner petals are called "standards," and are usually erect and arching. The edges of the flower parts are often ruffled or laced.

The vast range of colors and color combinations have resulted in a specialized terminology for the plant. Generally, the flowers are divided into five categories:

1. A *self* is a flower with solid, uniform color.

2. A *plicata* is generally white or yellow, with contrasting "freckles," or mottling.

3. A *bicolor* has standards of one color and falls of another, usually darker color. Bicolors have several subclasses, including: *amoenas*, which have white standards and colored falls; *reverse amoenas*, with white falls and colored standards; and *variegatas*, which have yellow standards and falls of purple, red, or brown.

4. *Bitones* have standards of one color, and falls of a different value of the same color.

5. *Blends*, the last category, are varieties with two or more colors variously intergraded in the same flower parts.

Bearded iris usually bloom for 2 to 3 weeks in April, May, or June, depending upon the variety.

The gray-green leaves are held stiffly erect in a fanlike pattern. Tall stems arise from the foliage, branching toward the top to produce blooms on short pedicels.

The plants spread by rhizomes, producing large, indefinitely expanding clumps that tend to decline and die out in the center unless periodically divided. Each plant "rests" for a few weeks after blooming, during which time excessive feeding may be detrimental. The leaf tips tend to brown in the summer after blooming, especially in dry years.

How to start: Nursery stock or division of rhizomes are the preferred methods. Division should be done after flowering is complete, but not later than mid-August. The rhizomes should be separated so that each division has one fan of leaves and several feeder roots. Set the rhizome so that the top is 1 inch below the soil surface, and the newest leaves (and main direction of growth) face the direction in which you

Iris 'Graphic Arts'
(bearded hybrid)

Iris 'Broadway'
(bearded hybrid)

Iris kaempferi

want the plant to grow. Cut the leaves back to 6 inches after planting. Sowing seed is a complex and intriguing undertaking for those gardeners interested in selecting and breeding.

Where to plant: Bearded iris must have well-drained soil, preferably of neutral pH, fertile, and fairly high in organic matter. Give it full sun for the best flowering. Space plants 12 to 15 inches apart. Hardy to zone 3.

Care: Moderately difficult. Water adequately but never allow the soil to remain soggy. Tall bearded iris are heavy feeders; feed once heavily in the early spring, and again at about half the strength 4 or 5 weeks after blooming has finished. Remove all spent flowers or developing seed pods regularly.

Iris borer is a serious pest, inflicting severe damage and providing entrance for bacterial soft rot. Begin an insecticide program in spring when leaves are 2 to 3 inches tall, and repeat weekly for the next 2 to 3 weeks. Infected rhizomes should be removed and destroyed. Remove old foliage and litter in the fall as it may harbor borer eggs. The presence of borers can often be spotted by attentive gardeners before damage is noticeable. Watch for the trails of slime they leave along the leaf edge before tunneling down through the central portion of a fan into the rhizome.

Plants should be divided every third or fourth year for rejuvenation. Division is also the best means of increase, and is best done just after blooming is complete, when the plant enjoys a brief dormancy. It can also be done in early spring, but this may delay flowering until the following year.

Varieties: Several hundred varieties are introduced each year, and available cultivars number in the thousands.

Iris kaempferi
and hybrids
(Japanese Iris)
Iris family. Native to Japan.

Massive, stately foliage and huge, flat blossoms distinguish this iris. It is quite finicky about location, but once established in moist, acid soil, needs little attention for a long, colorful life.

The flowers are white, blue, purple, lavender, and pink. They are often 6 inches or more across. The three overlapping outer falls (see page 76) are large, flat, and held horizontally, and the inner standards are small and spreading. They bloom in late June and July.

The dark green, swordlike leaves often grow 3 to 4 feet tall, and remain attractive all season. They are graceful, upright, and slightly arching in clusters topped by tall flowering stems. Stems usually grow 3 to 4 feet high, and heights of 6 feet are not uncommon in rich, boggy soil in mild climates.

Japanese iris are restrained in growth and long-lived. Their rhizomes gradually expand to form a clump.

How to start: Nursery stock or division or rhizomes in spring are the accepted methods. Set the divisions 1 inch below the soil level.

Where to plant: The soil must be acid, very moist, and well supplied with organic matter. The plant tolerates and even thrives in boggy or frequently flooded areas. Lime and alkaline soil are usually fatal. Give them either full sun or partial shade. Space plants 18 to 24 inches apart. Hardy to zone 4.

Care: Moderately easy. Water abundantly and maintain acid soil conditions. Feed occasionally with acid plant food. This plant has no serious pests. Division is rarely needed for rejuvenation; most plants can be left undis-

turbed indefinitely. It is an exellent means of increase, however, and is best performed in spring, although it can be done in late summer after flowering.

Related species and varieties: Many hybrids are available in white, reddish purple, rose, lavender, blue, violet, purple, and various combinations thereof.

Iris pseudacorus (Water Flag Iris) is another large beardless iris that prefers very moist, acid conditions. The flowers are yellow and appear in great quantities atop 36- to 40-inch stems. This iris will self-sow prolifically in boggy, wet locations, and has become naturalized in many such areas in North America.

Iris
Pacific Coast species and hybrids
(Pacific Coast Iris)
Iris family. Native to coastal western North America.

The Pacific Coast iris resembles a small Siberian iris, to which it is closely related. The delicate, open blossoms are available in a wide array of colors, and they have handsome, grasslike, evergreen leaves. They are most suited to coastal gardens where the summers are mild, especially in the West, where they thrive in the wet winters and dry summers.

The flowers are available in a wide range of colors from white to blue, violet, purple, rose, tangerine, orange, yellow, bronze, and brown, usually solid, but sometimes mottled. The falls (see page 76) are frequently wider and more rounded than in the Siberian iris, are held horizontally, and in many varieties are richly veined or blotched with a contrasting color. The standards, rather than being held vertically, open crisply to an angle. The flowers bloom

Iris 'Amaquita'
(Pacific Coast hybrid)

Iris sibirica 'Sparkle'

in late March or April in mild climates, or May in more northern areas.

The deep green, linear leaves are arched and rather relaxed in appearance. They are produced singly, rather than in a fan, and form solid, tight, grasslike clumps. They are evergreen and generally handsome all year long, although they may become browned at the tips toward the end of the summer dormancy period.

The plant has many branched flowering stems, which hold the flowers within or slightly above the foliage. Most varieties rarely exceed 12 to 18 inches high.

Pacific Coast iris may occasionally reseed in optimum environments, but this is seldom a problem and they are never invasive. They hybridize freely, and extreme variation will result from plants grown from seed. Pacific Coast iris spread by surface rhizomes, and their slow growth results in a gradual expansion of the clumps.

How to start: Nursery stock or divisions are preferred. Division is best done in late summer or fall, but can be successful in spring just after flowering.

Where to plant: Native to areas of mild, wet winters and temperate, dry summers, if planted in hot, wet-summer areas they must have perfect drainage and light shade to survive. They prefer well-drained soil high in organic matter and of only moderate fertility. In coastal climates, full sun is best. Space plants 10 to 18 inches apart. Hardy to zone 6, possibly southern zone 5.

Care: These iris require little attention. Fertilize only lightly in early spring. Remove spent flowers and developing seed pods. Do not water during the summer dormancy. The plant has no serious pests. Division is best

performed in fall (September in the East, October or November in the West), but can be successful in spring after flowering. It is rarely required for rejuvenation.

Iris sibirica
and hybrids
(Siberian Iris)
Iris family. Native to central Europe and Russia.

Exceptional hardiness, easy culture, long life, and durable, handsome foliage rank the Siberian iris as first rate for the border or landscape. All have narrow, linear, almost grasslike leaves of various heights, that support delicate flowers in June.

Shades of white, blue, and purple are the dominant flower colors now, but new hybridization work promises a much wider selection in the near future. The flowers are smaller and more delicate than those of the bearded iris. The three standards are erect, and the three falls are not bearded (see page 76). The blooms have an open quality and are borne in generous quantities on long stems that are somewhat branched toward the top.

The bright, dark green leaves can be as narrow as a half inch. They are clean and attractive all season long, and appear more relaxed than bearded iris foliage. Erect to arching clumps support many flower stems, with blossoms visible just above the leaves.

Depending upon variety, Siberian iris range from 18 to 36 inches tall. The small rhizomes and deep tangled roots expand outward slowly to form dense clumps. The plant seldom needs division, is not invasive, and can be very long-lived.

How to start: Nursery stock and divisions. Spring is the recommended time for division and planting, although it is usually successful throughout the summer.

Where to plant: The plant tolerates a wide range of soils, from extremely moist and rich to very poor and dry. They perform best, however, in moist, fertile soil of slight acidity. Give them full sun to partial shade; they will not flower well in deep shade. Space plants 18 to 24 inches apart. Hardy to zone 2.

Care: Easy. Provide abundant moisture and occasional feeding. To improve the plant's appearance, fastidious gardeners often remove spent flowers after blooming is complete. Although the plant is troubled by few pests, the iris borer can be a problem, contrary to some sources. Dig any infected plants, cut out and destroy the infected portions, and replant the remainder.

Division is rarely necessary for rejuvenation, but occasionally an old clump will become too crowded and start dying out in the center. Division can be difficult, as the clumps develop quite deep and dense roots. It is an excellent means of increase, however. It is best done in spring, but can be successful up to late summer.

Related species and varieties: Many hybrids of Siberian iris are available, mostly crosses between *Iris sanguinea* and *I. sibirica*. While too numerous to list here, the numbers are not nearly so overwhelming as with bearded iris.

Spuria iris is a class of beardless Eurasian species, some of which grow 4 feet tall. Their rhizomes have a creeping habit and can spread quite wide; they rarely form dense, crowded clumps. *I. orientalis* is the most commonly grown species, with bright yellow, delicate, butterfly blossoms generously produced on 40-inch stalks. The leaves are nar-

Liatris spicata

row, dark green, and handsome all season, except in hot, dry climates, where they die to the ground in midsummer. Many hybrids are continually being listed, ranging in size from 12 inches to 6 feet, and displaying a wide variety of flower colors in white, yellow, blue, violet, and bronze. Spuria iris are generally thought to be more tender than Siberians, and may need winter protection north of zone 6.

Kniphofia uvaria
and hybrids
formerly *Tritoma*
(Torch Lily; Red-Hot Poker)
Lily family. Native to South Africa.

The torch lily produces gracefully arching mounds of grasslike leaves and rigid, erect spikes of brilliant flowers that lend an exotic, almost tropical effect to the garden.

The flowers are flaming red or red-orange, blending into yellow below. The species bloom in August and September, the hybrids in June, July, or August. The plant is hardy only to zone 7, but many hybrids have been developed that extend and soften the color range and also are much hardier, often to zone 5 if mulched in winter.

The medium- to gray-green foliage forms dense tufted mounds that either arch gracefully or, in some varieties, are rigid. It is effective all season, and is evergreen in mild climates. The mounds are 12 to 30 inches high. From these arise the stiff, vertical "pokers," which can reach from 2 to 4 feet tall.

By producing young offshoots at the outer margins the clumps expand outward to about 3 to 3½ feet across in 4 or 5 years. The plant is long-lived.

How to start: Best purchased as container-grown nursery plants and planted in early spring. Or plant divisions in early spring.

Where to plant: The soil must be well drained; soggy conditions are usually deadly. Avoid windy spots, as taller spikes may get damaged or broken, and they are difficult to stake attractively. Give the plant full sun only. Space plants 18 inches apart.

Care: Easy. Mulch over winter where temperatures drop to 0° and below. There are no serious pests. Division may be needed every fourth or fifth year, but most clumps can go indefinitely without disturbance. Divide in early spring for increase. Either remove the young side growths individually, or dig the entire plant and divide the center clump.

Varieties: Many are available in white, cream, yellow, gold, pink, coral red, orange, and scarlet. Among the hardiest are 'Earliest of All', coral rose in June; 'Springtime', coral-red and white; and 'Summer Sunshine', flame red.

Liatris spicata
(Blazing Star; Gayfeather)
Daisy family. Native to eastern North America.

Tall rose, lavender, or purple flower spikes make this plant a useful vertical accent for the garden. Use it either singly in the mixed border, or in groups of three or more.

The individual flowers resemble tiny thistle blooms and are packed densely along the upper 12 to 30 inches of the stems. Blooming in July to September, they open over time from the top of the spike to the bottom.

The dark green, almost grasslike leaves are up to 16 inches long at the base of the plant and become smaller toward the top. They are stemless and arranged alternately along the flower stalk.

Blazing star can grow from 2 to 5 feet tall, although 3 feet is most usual in cultivation. Height varies widely depending upon growing conditions and heredity. The plant often self-sows but is seldom invasive. The clumps expand slowly by sending up new stems about the base. It is long-lived.

How to start: The easiest method is to sow seeds outdoors in early spring or summer. Seeds must first be prechilled in the refrigerator for several weeks. Germination takes 15 days or more. Due to variability, named cultivars should be started by divisions made in spring, or from nursery plants.

Where to plant: Native to wet meadows and marsh edges in eastern North America, this species responds to moist, well-drained soil high in organic matter and of moderate fertility. In wet locations it may self-sow prolifically. Give it full sun. Space plants 12 to 15 inches apart. Hardy to zone 3.

Care: Easy. Water abundantly. Removing spent flower spikes may promote a secondary bloom on lateral stems. When cutting a flowering stem, leave two-third for the plant's food production. It has few pests. In areas where the southern root-knot nematode is known to be a problem, the plant should be avoided.

Crowded plants may require division every third or fourth year, but most can go many years without needing rejuvenation. For increase, divide in early spring.

Ligularia 'The Rocket'

Lobelia cardinalis

Lupinus
'Russell Hybrids'

Related species and varieties: *Liatris spicata* 'Kobold' is an 18- to 24-inch dwarf with deep purple flowers.

L. scariosa (Tall Gayfeather) can grow from 18 inches to 5 feet high. It is best known for its selections 'September Glory', a deep purple in color; and 'White Spires', in white. Both have tall flower spikes that open simultaneously instead of gradually from top to bottom. This species is native to sandy prairies and must have very well-drained soil that remains fairly dry over winter.

Ligularia dentata
(Golden Groundsel)
Daisy family. Native to China and Japan.

Large, bold leaves and tall spires of flowers make golden groundsel a useful specimen or border plant.

The small flowers are orange-yellow to bright yellow, about 2 inches across, and appear in large quantities held tightly against the tall flower stalks. They bloom in August.

The deep green leaves have a purplish tint. They are broad, rounded, somewhat heart-shape, and grow up to 12 inches across. They are effective all season, but are prone to drooping and wilting in hot sun and during periods of high heat and humidity.

The plant forms dense basal clumps of leaves up to 18 inches high. From these arise 30- to 40-inch stiffly vertical flower stalks. Clumps expand at a moderate rate through the growth of short rhizomes. The plant is fairly restrained in growth and is long-lived.

How to start: Divisions or nursery plants in spring are best.

Where to plant: Moist, rich soil high in organic matter. Dry soils are quickly fatal, but the plants also resent sogginess. Partial shade is best, but the plant tolerates full sun, especially in cool climates and moist soil. Hot sun causes unsightly drooping of foliage, especially in humid weather. Space plants 24 inches apart. Hardy to zone 4.

Care: Moderately easy. Water abundantly. Feed regularly. Bait for slugs and snails. Division is rarely necessary. It is best performed in spring.

Lobelia cardinalis
(Cardinal Flower)
Lobelia family. Native to eastern North America.

The cardinal flower is a tall, stately plant with brilliant scarlet flowers in mid to late summer. It is a fine choice for moist, shady spots, especially in natural gardens.

The individual flowers are small and grow in a spike along the upper 6 or 8 inches of the stem. They are attractive to hummingbirds, and bloom in late July to September.

The medim or dark green leaves are oblong or lance-shape, growing to 4 inches long. They are arranged oppositely or in whorls along the stalks. The tall, vertical stems grow 3 to 4 feet high, and are topped with the blazing red flowers.

Unfortunately, the cardinal flower is short-lived. It will self-sow under optimum conditions, but this is difficult to rely on. It is seldom, if ever, invasive.

How to start: It is easiest to plant nursery stock or sow seed outdoors in late fall. Or, in late fall divide and plant new shoots that form around the base of the plant.

Where to plant: Native to wet soils along streams and in meadows or to woodland bottomlands, cardinal flower is best in well-drained, sandy loam high in organic matter and kept evenly moist. While tolerant of full sun if soil is kept moist, it is best in shade or partial shade. Space plants 12 to 18 inches apart. Hardy to zone 2. It does not perform well in regions of mild winters.

Care: Moderately difficult. Keep the plant well watered. Remove faded flower stalks. Mulch in summer to retain moisture, and in winter to protect the crowns. Although several insects and fungal diseases can attack the plant, they are seldom serious enough to warrant protection. The plant should be divided annually to perpetuate it. Lift the clump, then remove and reset the outside clusters of new basal growth. This is best done in the early fall.

Lupinus
'Russell Hybrids'
(Russell Lupines)
Pea family. Hybrids of uncertain parentage.

These huge, spiky racemes of flowers, available in nearly every color and combination of colors, are unfortunately adapted only to cool-summer, humid climates. Where they can be grown, they are outstanding either in the mixed border or massed in beds all to themselves.

Many types of lupine are bicolored, and most are available only as mixes. Individually the flowers are pealike,

and are arranged in tight whorls that encircle the stem, creating clusters that are 1 to 2 feet long. Lending a strong vertical effect to the garden, they bloom in June.

The dark green, compound leaves are from 2 to 6 inches across and radiate out like the palm of a hand. They are produced on 6- to 12-inch stalks. Dense with foliage and bushy at the base, each plant sends up several flowering spikes.

In favorable climates lupines will self-sow profusely, but the progeny usually revert back to blue or white colors. Clumps tend to expand and crowd, necessitating division, if the plants live long enough. They are relatively short-lived, but can persist long in the garden—to the point of being invasive—due to reseeding.

How to start: Easiest started from seed, but they do require hand-pollinated seed, which can be expensive. Nick the seed coats or soak the seeds for 24 hours prior to sowing. Sow outdoors in place in spring or late summer, or indoors 8 to 10 weeks prior to setting out in early spring. Indoors, they will germinate in 4 to 5 weeks with 75° night temperatures and 80° days. Move them outside carefully, as they resent transplanting. Sowing in peat pots is the best method. Applying an inoculant for nitrogen-fixing bacteria to wetted seeds reportedly results in a more robust seedling. The plants also can be started from nursery stock or by division.

Where to plant: Best in climates with cool, mild summers and high humidity. They prefer a neutral, well-drained soil of only moderate fertility. Give them full sun or partial shade. Space plants 18 to 24 inches apart. Hardy to zone 3.

Care: Particular about climate; but otherwise easy. Remove spent flowers before they can set seed. Mulch to retain moisture and keep roots cool. Water over dry periods. A light mulch in areas of harsh winters can be helpful. A regular program of insecticide and fungicide will help protect the plant from powdery mildew, rust, aphids, and the four-lined plant bug. Division is rarely necessary as the plants are short-lived. For increase, divide in early spring.

Lychnis chalcedonica

(Maltese Cross)
Pink family. Native to the northern Soviet Union.

The small flowers of this plant are curiously shaped like a cross. They are brilliant scarlet-orange and are gathered into dense, rounded clusters atop 2-foot vertical stems. Rose and white cultivars are also available.

The individual flowers are small and five-petaled. They bloom in June and July. Consistent removal of spent flowers will encourage a secondary bloom in August.

The dark green, slightly hairy leaves are held at right angles to the stems. Leaves at the base are longest, to 4 or 5 inches, shrinking to 2 inches at the top. Dense clumps of straight, vertical stems 1 to 2 feet tall support the flower clusters.

Maltese cross will reseed, and can become an invasive nuisance. It is generally short-lived. If it lives long enough, the clump will expand gradually by sending up new shoots around the base; it can become overcrowded and need division.

How to start: Best started from seed sown outdoors in spring, summer, or fall. It will flower the first year if started early indoors, germinating in 3 to 4 weeks at a temperature of 70°. Do not cover the seeds, as they respond to light. Seedlings are difficult to transplant, so start them in peat pots. The plant can also be started by nursery plants or by divisions made in spring or fall.

Where to plant: Soil must be perfectly drained; wet soil in winter generally is fatal. Give it full sun. Space plants 12 to 15 inches apart. Hardy to zone 3.

Care: Moderately difficult. Remove spent flowers to encourage a longer bloom season and a secondary bloom in August. Leaf spot, root rot (particularly in winter-wet soil), rust, and smut can all be problems. A regular fungicide program would be helpful. Divide in spring or fall every third or fourth year, as the clumps become overcrowded.

Related species and varieties: *Lychnis coronaria* (Rose Campion) is a biennial with brilliant magenta flowers produced singly on silvery gray stems and leaves. The plants present an open, stretchy feeling. Although biennial, it will self-sow with tremendous vitality. Plant one in your garden and its progeny will be around forever.

Lychnis haageana (Haage Campion), despite its hybrid origin, still reproduces well from seed. The flowers are the same scarlet orange, but are larger and appear singly at the ends of the stems.

Lysimachia punctata

Lysimachia clethroides

Lysimachia clethroides
(Gooseneck Loosestrife)
Primrose family. Native to China and Japan.

Vigorous and easy, these bushy, spreading perennials produce flower spikes shaped like a goose's neck. The leafy, dense clumps are effective as a low background, and the white flowers are an attractive addition to the late-summer border.

The individual flowers are minute and grouped in dense spikes 6 to 8 inches long. The spikes are conical, relaxed, and bent at the ends into a graceful, S-shape curve. They bloom in July and August.

The medium green, slightly hairy leaves are of medium texture and turn an attractive bronze-yellow in the fall. The clumps of erect to slightly spreading stems have a bushy appearance and grow up to 3 feet high.

The plant spreads rapidly and can become invasive if not divided regularly. It is long-lived.

How to start: The easiest method is sowing seed in early spring. You can also plant divisions made in spring, or nursery plants.

Where to plant: Best in moist, rich soil high in organic matter. Drier soils are tolerated in partial shade. In moist soils give it full sun or partial shade. Space plants 15 to 24 inches apart. Hardy to zone 3.

Care: Easy. Water abundantly. Crown rot and white fly have been reported as problems. The plant can go for years before needing rejuvenation, but division is usually required every 2 to 4 years to restrain the size of the clump. It is best done in the spring.

Related species and varieties: *Lysimachia nummelaria* (Moneywort) is a low, creeping plant generally reserved as a ground cover. Entirely different in appearance from gooseneck loosestrife, it bears brilliant yellow flowers in June through August. Like its relative, it can be extremely invasive, especially in moist soils and around well-watered lawns. It is very well adapted to wet, boggy conditions and shade.

L. punctata (Yellow Loosestrife) produces long, 3-foot, vertical stems covered with whorls of yellow flowers in June and early July. It can be invasive unless restrained, but is a sturdy and reliable plant.

Lythrum salicaria
(Purple Loosestrife)
Loosestrife family. Native to Europe.

The purple loosestrife is an excellent example of the perils of common names, for it is unrelated to the previously described plant, gooseneck loosestrife, and also considerably different in appearance and behavior.

Purple loosestrife is a tall, bushy plant that produces erect stems covered with bright flowers nearly all summer. It can reseed quite rampantly in boggy situations, but is usually quite restrained in growth in the border.

The flowers are pink, magenta, reddish purple, or deep purple. Individually they are about an inch across, and are produced densely along erect, 12- to 15-inch spikes. They bloom in July to September.

The medium green leaves are lance-shape and 2 to 4 inches long. They are produced sparsely in whorls along the stems. The stems are strong, almost woody, multibranched, and erect, growing 3 to 5 feet tall. Flowers appear on the top 8 to 15 inches of the stems. The overall form is a vase shape.

Although the hybrid cultivars do not seem to be so rampant, the species will reseed in wet areas. It has naturalized abundantly in the East, frequently choking out large areas of vegetation in swampy areas or around bodies of water. These plants are long-lived, gradually expanding into large clumps by continually producing basal shoots.

How to start: Easy to start by seed sown in spring or fall. Germination takes about 2 weeks. The cultivars, which are generally superior, should be started by nursery plants or divisions made in spring. Seed-grown plants will vary considerably.

Where to plant: Although purple loosestrife is best adapted to moist, shady areas, it will perform perfectly well in ordinary garden soil and full sun. Space plants 24 inches apart. Hardy to zone 3.

Care: Easy. Water abundantly for the best effect. Removing faded blossoms will improve appearance, possibly extend the flowering season, and prevent self-sowing. The plant has no serious pests. It can go many years before requiring division for rejuvenation. Division is the best means of increase for cultivars. Divide either in spring or fall. Use a sharp knife, because the dense, woody roots can be difficult to separate.

Lythrum salicaria
'Morden's Pink'

Mertensia virginica

Monarda didyma
'Granite Pink'

Mertensia virginica

(Virginia Bluebells)
Borage family. Native to the eastern
United States.

The Virginia bluebells have drooping,
bell-shape flowers that appear in
spring. The erect, leafy plants are most
attractive in the informal or wild
garden.

The outer portion of the petals is sky
blue and the inner part pinkish or purplish. Each flower is about an inch long,
and they are produced in clusters that
hang gracefully at the ends of branching stems. They bloom in April and
May.

The medium green leaves are produced both in basal rosettes and alternately along the stems. Leaves are
about 8 inches long at the base, becoming smaller as they ascend the stems.
All foliage dies back and usually has
disappeared by July.

The stems, which reach 12 to 24
inches high, are gracefully relaxed and
curved at the tips. The plant overall is
erect and slightly spreading. Long-lasting in suitable locations, Virginia blue-
bell is restrained in growth and not
invasive, but will self-sow here and
there.

How to start: Easily started from
seed sown outside in early spring or
fall, from nursery plants, or from the
division of dormant roots in early fall.
When planting divisions, set the crowns
1 inch below the soil level.

Where to plant: The plant prefers a
cool, moist soil high in organic matter;
and is partial to deep shade. It does
best in cool-summer climates of northern latitudes. Space them 8 to 12 inches
apart. Hardy to zone 3.

Care: Easy, in the right location.
Mulching will help keep soil cool and
moist in the summer and also provide a
continual supply of decaying organic
matter. Keep the soil evenly moist but
never soggy. Do not remove the foliage
when it starts to degenerate, but allow
it to die down naturally, as with bulbs.
Some fungal diseases have been reported, but the plant generally is little
troubled by disease or pests. Division is
seldom required other than for increase. It should always be performed
in early fall when roots are dormant.

Monarda didyma

(Bee Balm)
Mint family. Native to the eastern
United States.

Bee balm's vigorous, bushy clusters of
erect stems are topped with fluffy,
dense flower heads in shades of pink,
purple, white, or red. They will attract
hummingbirds, bees, and butterflies to
your garden in profusion.

The individual flowers are small and
tubular, arranged in single or double
whorls into the rounded flower heads.
Reddish-colored cultivars are especially
attractive to hummingbirds. The plant
blooms in late June and into August.

The dark green, lance-shape leaves
are perpendicular to the stem and opposite one another. Like other members of the mint family, they have a
slightly crinkled texture and are aromatic when crushed. They are dense,
lush, and remain attractive all season.
The dense clumps of erect to slightly
spreading stems grow 2 to 3 feet tall.

Bee balm spreads rapidly, and sometimes invasively, to form dense mats of
fibrous, shallow roots. With age the
stems become sparse, lanky, and tall,
unless regularly divided.

How to start: Named varieties are
generally superior to the species, and
are best started by nursery plants or divisions planted in spring. The species
is easy to start from seed sown outdoors
in spring or fall. Or sow indoors in
early spring at 65°. Germination takes 1
to 2 weeks.

Where to plant: Best in moist soil
high in organic matter and of only average fertility. Give it full sun. In shady
locations and rich soil it can become
extremely vigorous and spread rampantly. Space 24 inches apart. Hardy to
zone 4.

Care: Moderately easy. Water abundantly for best appearance, but with-
hold fertilizer to forestall rapid
spreading. Bee balm has few serious
pests. In crowded situations with poor
air circulation, several fungus problems,
such as powdery mildew and rust, may
occur. Although many sources recom-
mend spring division as best, with care
bee balm may be moved successfully almost anytime. The clumps will need
division every 3 to 4 years for contain-
ment and rejuvenation. This is also an
excellent means of increase.

Varieties: 'Cambridge Scarlet' has
flaming scarlet flowers and is one of the
best and most popular
varieties.'Croftway Pink' has soft, rosy-
pink flowers that fade to lavender.
Other frequently offered cultivars are
'Snow Queen', with white flowers, and
'Blue Stocking', with light purple
flowers.

Paeonia 'Janice'

Papaver orientalis

Paeonia
hybrids
(Herbaceous Peony)
Peony family. The parentage of the many hybrids is uncertain, but most are native to Eurasia, a few to North America.

Incredibly long-lived, with huge, fragrant flowers available in a vast array of colors and forms, as well as glossy foliage that is attractive all season, the peony is considered by many to be indispensable for the border. Its neat, bushy shape and easy culture make it also a valuable addition to the landscape.

Flowers come in shades of pink, white, red, and yellow. They are large, 3 to 6 inches across, and sit atop long stems ideal for cutting. They bloom in May and June.

Five basic peony flower forms are recognized

1. *Doubles* are fluffy, almost spheroid flowers in which the stamens have developed into fully petal-like structures.

2. *Semidoubles* are similar, but in these the stamens are not quite so fully developed.

3. The *Japanese* form is characterized by one or more rows of petals surrounding stamens that carry no pollen, and hence are the same color as the petals.

4. The *anemone* form is similar to the Japanese except that the stamens have been transformed into narrow, petal-like parts.

5. *Singles* have one or more rows of petals that surround a mass of golden stamens.

The leaves are a deep, glossy green, deeply lobed, and medium in texture. The emerging young shoots are reddish and very attractive in spring; and the leaves occasionally develop crimson tints in the fall.

Many leafy shoots appear from a central clump of fleshy roots, creating a bushy, rounded shape that can grow to 3 feet tall. The clumps expand gradually to spread as wide. Peonies are long-lived, restrained in growth, and neat.

How to start: From nursery plants or by divisions planted in August or September.

Where to plant: Peonies need a deep, rich, well-drained loam generously amended with organic matter. Full sun is generally best, although light shade is tolerated well. The latter is probably best for pastel shades that will fade quickly in hot sun. Space plants 2 to 3 feet apart when massing, 3 to 4 feet apart as specimens. Hardy to zone 5. It does not perform well in subtropical regions of the Southwest and Southeast, apparently requiring some winter cold.

Care: Usually easy. Water adequately, especially during dry spells. Feed annually in the spring, but never allow fresh manure or fast-acting nitrogen to directly contact the fleshy roots.

Bait for snails and slugs in the spring, as the emerging shoots are particularly vulnerable. Botrytis and Phytophthora blights are the major problems. Practice good garden sanitation by removing and destroying the old foliage in the fall; and prevent water from standing on the foliage in the cool of the evening. Regular applications of fungicide during bud and bloom may help to prevent botrytis blight.

Division is best accomplished in late August or September. Lift the plants and, with a sharp knife, separate the fleshy roots into segments that each have three to five eyes (the reddish buds visible at the top of the roots). Plant the sections so that the eyes face up and are *exactly* 1 inch below the soil surface.

Varieties: Literally thousands of cultivars are available.

Papaver orientalis
(Oriental Poppy)
Poppy family. Native to Southwest Asia.

Oriental poppies produce large, crepe-papery flowers, and coarse, toothed foliage. They grow best in regions of cool summers, and are best used in conjunction with late-appearing plants that can take over in late summer.

Originally, scarlet-orange was the only available color of oriental poppies; but now a wide variety of pinks, reds, oranges, and whites can be found. Most varieties have black splotches and black stamens in the center of the blossom. The flowers are from 4 to 10 inches across, and have a rumpled texture. They are borne singly at the ends of long, hairy stems. They bloom in June.

The light green or grayish leaves are large and hairy. They are dense at the base of the plant, smaller and more scarce higher up. The foliage dies down and disappears in July and August, but new growth often appears in September and persists over the winter. The foliage supports many flower stems that reach 2 to 4 feet high. The stems have a serpentine, curving quality.

Penstemon hartwegii
'Evelyn'

Phlox paniculata

Poppies are fairly long-lived as long as the soil is well drained. The clumps of foliage expand gradually and can reach 3 feet wide. They should be interplanted with other plants to compensate for the vacant spots left by the dying foliage.

How to start: Nursery plants or divisions. Divisions should be planted from August to early September. Set the root crowns 3 inches below the soil level. Mulch lightly over the first winter but guard against suffocating the young crowns.

Where to plant: The plant must have well-drained soil; wet crowns, particularly in winter, are usually fatal. Adding organic matter can be beneficial, but the soil should be of only average fertility. It performs best in regions of cool summers, and is short-lived in warm-winter climates. Give it full sun or partial shade. Space plants 15 to 20 inches apart. Hardy to zone 2.

Care: Moderately easy, with excellent drainage. A summer mulch will help keep the soil cool and the roots moist. Take care not to damage roots with cultivation in late summer after the foliage has died down. Plants with tall stems probably will require staking.

Avoid letting water stand on leaves and crowns on cool days or overnight, as this invites bacterial blight and downy mildew. Aphids may present a problem, as may the northern root-knot nematode.

Oriental poppies will require division every 4 or 5 years for rejuvenation. This is best done in August or early September.

Varieties: Over sixty cultivars are commonly sold.

Penstemon hartwegii
(Beardtongue)
Snapdragon family. Native to Mexico.

Penstemons produce colorful, trumpet-like blossoms of rose, pink, lavender, or white that are vaguely similar to snapdragons or foxgloves. Members of the genus grow naturally from Oregon to Chile; thus, they are most suited to mild coastal and other humid climates with temperate winters. In cold areas they are treated as annuals.

The flowers are tubular and about 2 inches long. They are arranged in open spikes and nod on slender pedicels. They bloom in June and July.

The medium-green, lance-shape, almost linear leaves are 2 to 4 inches long. The stems are vertical, branching at the base. The structure is like an open, loose-flowered and bushy snapdragon. The plants grow from 1 to 3 feet tall, depending upon variety.

Somewhat delicate in nature, beard-tongue generally is not long-lived. It will self-sow in a favorable climate, but the seedlings will be quite variable.

How to start: Nursery plants or by sowing hand-pollinated seeds outdoors in late summer. Seeds may be sown indoors in early spring at 65°. Germination usually takes less than a week. Division in spring is possible, but more difficult.

Where to plant: The soil must be well-drained and gritty, and preferably on the acid side (pH 5.5 to 6.5). Full sun is best, but it tolerates light shade. Space plants 12 to 18 inches apart. Penstemon should be considered only for mild, coastal climates. Hardy to zone 7.

Care: Moderately difficult; the plant is particular about location. Do not overwater, but be sure to water adequately during droughts. Most members of the genus are native to mild-winter, dry-summer climates of the Mediterranean and the western Americas. To prevent seed formation, cut the stems after flowering. Do not overfertilize. Mulch over winter to protect from cold. The plant has no serius pests, although leaf spot and rust have been reported. Fungicide is an effective protection. While difficult to transplant, many cultivars will require division every other year to look their best. This is best done in early spring.

Phlox paniculata
(Summer Phlox; Garden Phlox)
Phlox family. Native to the eastern United States.

Massive color and stately appearance are the hallmarks of this perennial phlox. Equally characteristic is the need for spraying, staking, frequent watering and dividing, and weeding out self-sown seedlings. Despite the work in raising phlox well, many gardeners consider it indispensable for the border.

Flowers come in red, pink, salmon, magenta, purple, lavender, and white. Individually they are like discs about 1 inch across and are gathered into massive conical or hemispherical flower heads 10 to 14 inches across. They usually bloom in July to early September, but this varies according to cultivar.

The dark green leaves are lance-shape and about 3 to 5 inches long. The 2- to 4-foot-high stems are dense with foliage, each topped with a large flower head.

Phlox subulata

Polygonatum commutatum
Platycodon grandiflorus 'Mariesii'

Phlox self-sows prolifically, but the seedlings of cultivars all revert back to their original magenta. This is a relatively short-lived plant. It requires thinning out of old growth annually, and division every third year.

How to start: Best results occur from nursery plants or divisions made in either spring or fall. Most cultivars purchased at nurseries are root cuttings. If started from seed, it should be sown in fall.

Where to plant: The soil should be deep, moist, well-drained, high in organic matter, and very fertile. It is best to add superphosphate generously to the soil when planting. Full sun is best, although the plant tolerates partial shade. Provide a location with good air circulation, but avoid windy spots. Space plants 24 inches apart. Hardy to zone 3.

Care: Difficult for a presentable appearance. Water abundantly, especially during drought, but do so early in the day and preferably from below to avoid getting water on the foliage. Fertilize regularly. Removing the flower heads, snapping them off just below the last flower, will encourage the formation of lateral buds, hence more flowers; it will also discourage reseeding. The plant will require staking.

Powdery mildew and rust, in addition to red spider mites in hot, dry weather, are the worst problems. Spray with insecticide and fungicide every 10 days to 2 weeks throughout the season.

Divide every third year to rejuvenate, but replant only the healthiest outer shoots of the clump. This should be done in either spring or fall.

Related species: *Phlox subulata* (Moss Pink) is an entirely different plant in appearance and care. It is low and mat-forming with bright green, dense, needlelike, evergreen leaves. It can make an excellent ground cover or bed in full sun and light, sandy soil. In early spring (April) it is covered with flowers in shades of pink, white, red, or lavender. The hues are usually of electric intensity. Moss pink is also hardy to zone 3.

Platycodon grandiflorus
(Balloon Flower)
Harebell family. Native to eastern Asia.

The balloon flower is a long-lived and easy perennial whose bell-shape blossoms resemble small inflated balloons when in bud.

Its flowers come in shades of blue (the usual color), white, and pink. They are 2 to 3 inches across, and appear at the ends of long stems in the upper part of the plant. They bloom in July and August, and often into early September.

The leaves are medium green with a bluish cast to the underside. They are oval to lance-shape, 1 to 3 inches long, and grow densely against the stems. The bushy clusters of erect stems are 2 to 3 feet tall. The flowers appear above and within the foliage.

Balloon flower is restrained in growth and long-lived. It is slow to appear in the spring, so be careful with early cultivation. It is also slow to achieve a mature clump; the full effect is seldom achieved before 3 years.

How to start: The plant can be started from seed, but flowers will not appear for 2 to 3 years. Sow seeds in spring or late summer, and do not cover them with soil. Divisions give

faster results, but the plant can be difficult to transplant. Cut off the outer sections of the thick crown, retaining as many buds and roots as possible, and plant these divisions thickly to safeguard against some failures. Set the crowns so that they are barely covered with soil.

Where to plant: Light, fluffy, sandy, and well-drained soil is best. The plant tolerates many soils, but will not take wet soil in winter. Give it either full sun or partial shade. Space plants 12 to 18 inches apart. Hardy to zone 3.

Care: Easy. The plant responds to adequate watering, but will flower well in hot, dry locations. Removing faded flowers will extend the bloom season. Tall plants may require staking. The plant has no serious pests. Division is often difficult and usually gives erratic results. Fortunately the plants are long-lived and never require division for rejuvenation. Dividing for propagation is best done in spring.

Polygonatum commutatum
(Great Solomon's Seal)
Lily family. Native to eastern North America.

This subtle woodland native has long, attractive, arching stems and hanging clusters of tiny flowers. It is one of those rare plants that will thrive in dry shade.

The flowers are yellowish green to greenish white, about ½ inch long, bell-shape, and droop in small clusters all along the undersides of the stems. They bloom in May and early June.

Foliage is the chief attraction of this plant. The deep, rich green to bluish-green leaves grow up to 7 inches long. They are held perpendicular to the stem and alternate along its length.

Primula vulgaris
'Barnhaven' hybrids

Primula cockburniana

Primula × polyanthes

The stems, which are unbranched, often reach 3 to 4 feet in length. The plant spreads slowly by rhizomes, and can form broad patches in time. It is long-lived and not invasive.

How to start: Nursery plants or divisions. Divisions should be planted in early spring or after flowering is complete.

Where to plant: Great Solomon's seal is best grown in cool, moist soil well amended with organic matter. However, it will tolerate dry soil and intensive root competition quite well. Give it deep to partial shade. Space plants 18 to 36 inches apart. Hardy to zone 4.

Care: Easy to moderately easy. Water adequately and mulch over summer. It has no serious pests. Although never required for rejuvenation, division for increase is easy when performed in early spring.

Primula vulgaris

(English Primrose)
Primrose family. Native to Europe.

Primula is a complex and varied genus of several hundred species, varying in height from a few inches to as much as 3 feet. Most bloom in April or May in northern climates, and as early as February in mild ones.

In general, primulas form basal rosettes of attractive, often crinkly, and sometimes evergreen leaves. From the foliage arise vertical flower stalks bearing single flowers, heads, or umbels, sometimes arranged in tiers. The flowers in the genus occur in all colors. *Primula vulgaris* and its hybrids are among the easiest to grow.

This plant's flowers are pale yellow. Hybrids are available in a wide range of nearly every color except pure red and pure blue. The flowers are about 1 inch

across, held one to a stalk just above the leaves. Prolific in bloom, a mature clump may produce more than a hundred flowers over a 2-month period.

The bright green leaves are tongue-like and produced in low basal rosettes, usually flat against the ground. They are evergreen where temperatures do not drop below 15°. Short flowering stalks grow from the center of the rosette.

Plants may go dormant in summer drought and re-emerge in autumn. They will self-sow in favorable environments, but are never invasive. Like most other primulas, this one spreads vegetatively, sending up new plantlets by way of surface roots near the crown. This primrose is fairly long-lived; however, frequent division is necessary to maintain vigor.

How to start: Easily grown from nursery bedding plants or from seed sown in late winter or early spring on the surface of a moist, peaty soil mix. The seeds require light to germinate and need humidity; so cover the flat with clear plastic. It is also easy to start from divisions made in spring after flowering is over, or in autumn.

Where to plant: Although many species are quite hardy, primroses grow best in mild, humid climates that do not have extreme summer or winter temperatures. Most, including this species, should have rich, deep, moist, well-drained soil high in organic matter. Partial shade, preferably the shade of high tree branches, is best. Protection from hot afternoon sun is essential. Space plants 6 to 15 inches apart. Hardy to zone 5.

Care: Moderately easy. Although particular about location, this is one of the easiest primroses to grow. Water abun-

dantly, especially during dry spells. Adding organic matter yearly by mulching over winter should provide all the nutrition it needs. It has no serious pests if kept vigorous. Clumps should be divided every third year to maintain vigor. Divide after flowering in the spring, or in the fall. Division is easy, and the plant quickly re-establishes itself.

Related species: *Primula × polyanthes* (Polyanthus Primrose) is the result of crosses made between *P. vulgaris* and several other species. This group is characterized by large, bold blooms, several to a stem, in a huge array of bright colors. Not as long-lived as *P. vulgaris*, they require essentially the same care. Division may be needed every other year, and occasional side-dressing with fertilizer is beneficial. In hot, dry weather, red spider mites can be a serious problem. Hardy to zone 5.

P. japonica (Japanese Primrose) is quite different in appearance, producing several tiers, or whorls, of magenta, pink, or white flowers along 2-foot stems. Like most of the candelabra types it requires a peaty, acid, and very moist or boggy soil, and can be difficult to grow if conditions are not exactly right. The blossoms begin to appear in May and often last through June. Other candelabra primroses are: *P. burmanica* and *P. beesiana*, both having purple flowers; *P. bulleyana* and *P. helodoxa*, yellow flowers; and *P. cockburniana* and *P.* 'Pagoda' hybrids, orange flowers. All require similar culture.

P. sieboldii has bright green, wrinkled leaves with scalloped edges and clusters of lilac-pink flowers on 6- to 9-inch stems in late spring. Hybrids are available in many shades of white, pink, and purple, including bicolors.

Rudbeckia fulgida
var. *sullivantii* 'Goldsturm'
with *Pennisetum alopecuriodes*

Pulmonaria saccharata

Pulmonaria saccharata
(Bethlehem Sage)
Borage family. Native to Europe.

The Bethlehem sage's deep green leaves speckled with white make an attractive ground cover in the shade. Small flowers in early spring are a decided extra advantage, and it is easy to grow.

Flowers come in blue, reddish violet, or white. Individually they are trumpet-like and about ½ inch long. They appear in relaxed clusters on stalks 10 to 12 inches tall. The flowers are often pink in bud, changing to blue as they open. They bloom in early April and May.

The exceedingly attractive, glossy leaves are oval to heart-shape, and grow to about 6 inches long. The basal rosettes of leaves reach 6 to 8 inches in height. From the crown arise several flowering stalks. The foliage remains attractive all season long.

The crowns gradually expand by producing more leaves at the outer edge of the clump. The plant is long-lived, restrained in growth, and not invasive.

How to start: Nursery plants or by divisions planted in fall or very early spring. Water full-planted divisions heavily until the ground freezes.

Where to plant: Moist soil high in organic matter is best, although it need not be fertile. Give these plants partial to deep shade. Space them 10 inches apart. Hardy to zone 4.

Care: Easy. The plant requires little attention. Watering over dry spells is beneficial. It has no serious pests. While seldom required, division is an excellent means of increase. It is best done in late summer or very early spring, although success is common even during full bloom. Water heavily after transplanting.

Related species and varieties: *Pulmonaria saccharata* 'Mrs. Moon' is a form with larger flowers that are pink in bud and bright blue when open.

P. angustifolia (Blue Lungwort) has plain dark green leaves that are quite hairy, almost bristly. The flowers are showy, pink in bud, opening to blue, and appear in April and May. Several varieties are available, including pink, salmon, white, and red ones. These may be listed under *P. saccharata* in some sources.

Rudbeckia fulgida
var. *sullivantii* 'Goldsturm'
(Goldsturm Black-eyed Susan)
Daisy family. Native to eastern North America.

Unlike many other members of this genus, this is a true, long-lived perennial that is not the least bit weedy. The deep yellow daisies of this plant are produced in great quantities over a long season in late summer. This cultivar is probably the best for its profuse bloom and its even, 2½-foot growth.

The flowers are deep yellow with a black central "cone." They are about 3 to 4 inches across, and nearly cover the plant over a long season, blooming from mid-July to mid-September. The cones persist and are attractive most of the winter.

The dark green, somewhat hairy leaves are lush and dense. The multi-branched stems are erect and spreading, usually growing to 30 inches tall. The overall form is a vase shape. The flowers are produced singly at the ends of the branches, often covering the foliage. Unlike most other rudbeckias, the foliage of this one remains clean and attractive all season.

Most black-eyed Susans are weedy self-sowers and are short-lived. This one is neither, having a restrained growth that will last for years in the garden. The clumps will expand gradually, sending up new shoots at the outer edges.

How to start: Nursery plants or division in spring are best. Fall planting too is generally successful.

Where to plant: Well-drained, moist soil of average fertility. The plant prefers full sun; in shade it will have an open habit and produce fewer flowers. Space 12 to 24 inches apart. Hardy to zone 4.

Care: Easy. Rudbeckia requires little attention and never needs staking. Water over dry periods. Aphids may be a problem, but are easily controlled with insecticide. Downy mildew, rust, and powdery mildew should be controlled with a fungicide. Division is best performed in spring, but is usually successful in fall as well. Most clumps will need dividing every fourth or fifth year to maintain their vigor.

Related species and varieties: *Rudbeckia hirta pulcherrima* 'Gloriosa Daisy' is often sold as a perennial, although in nearly all cases it behaves as a self-sowing annual.

R. laciniata 'Goldquelle' is like *R. fulgida* 'Goldsturm', except slower growing and with double flowers.

R. nitida 'Herbstonne' (usually listed as *R. nitida* 'Autumn Sun') grows 4 to 5 feet tall on strong stems that do not require staking. The flowers are deep yellow with brown centers, about 3 or 4 inches across, and are produced in generous quantities in late summer.

Salvia × superba
formerly *S. nemerosa*
(Perennial Salvia)
Mint family. Parents native to the Mediterranean region.

Spikes of violet-purple flowers and gray-green foliage that last throughout the season make this plant a welcome addition to the mixed border or individual beds.

The individual flowers are tiny and densely whorled around the spikes, which are 4 to 8 inches long. They bloom in June or August, and are surrounded by red-violet bracts that persist after the flowers are finished, providing a long, colorful season. The blooms are good for cut flowers and for drying for winter arrangements.

The leaves are of medium texture and effective all season long. They are aromatic when crushed. The multibranched stems are densely clothed in leaves, and the plant grows 2 to 3 feet tall.

Perennial salvia can be long-lived if conditions are favorable, especially if the soil is well drained. It stays in place and, since it is sterile, never self-sows.

How to start: By nursery plants, or by stem cuttings or divisions planted in spring.

Where to plant: The soil must be well-drained. Give it full sun. It will withstand heat, drought, and poor soil well. Wet soil in winter is usually fatal. Space plants 1 to 2 feet apart. An excellent choice for the southern states, it is hardy to zone 5, but success is frequent farther north with winter protection of snow or mulch.

Care: Easy in the right location. In northern zones apply a protective mulch after the soil freezes. Remove spent flowers to prolong the bloom period. Leaf spot, rust, scale, and white fly can be minor problems. Division is best done in spring. The root system is long and stringy, and re-establishment is usually slow. Fortunately, division is rarely required for rejuvenation.

Related species and varieties: *Salvia azurea* (Azure Sage) is a large, 4- to 5-foot plant with intense gentian-blue flowers in late summer and early fall. It is less hardy, to zone 6. Variety *grandiflora*, often listed in catalogs as *S. pitcheri*, has deeper, more brilliant blue flowers.

S. pratensis (Meadow Clary), formerly *S. haematodes*, is a multibranched plant with many flowering stems in lavender blue arising above a basal clump of foliage. It blooms in June. Because it often behaves as a biennial, it is wise to set out new plants yearly to perpetuate it in the garden, so that new plants are coming on each year.

Sedum 'Autumn Joy'
with *Yucca filamentosa* and
Calamagrostis epigeous in rear

Scabiosa caucasica

Scabiosa caucasica
(Pincushion Flower)
Teasel family. Native to the Caucasus.

The pincushion flower's pastel blue, sometimes white flowers on open, branching stems bloom nearly all summer long. Seldom planted as a focal specimen, it is an asset to the mixed, informal border.

The pale blue petals surround a hemisphere of protruding gray stamens that resemble pins in a pincushion. Growing to 3 inches across and appearing at the ends of the stems, they bloom in June to September.

The medium green basal leaves are oblong to lance-shape and measure up to 5 inches. The stem leaves are toothed and smaller. The foliage is large and dense at the base of the plant, becoming smaller and more sparse on the stems. The stems are upright and arching, and grow in clusters open and loose in appearance.

With periodic division, this is a relatively long-lived plant. It is restrained in habit. Clumps will expand gradually by sending up shoots at the outer perimeter.

How to start: Sow purchased seed in early spring, or sow indoors at 65°. Germination takes 1 to 2 weeks. It may bloom some by the end of the first season. Or sow freshly collected, ripe seed outdoors in early fall. Scabiosa may also be started by nursery plants or by planting divisions in spring.

Where to plant: Because summer drought and winter sogginess are both fatal, the plant requires the difficult-to-achieve combination of perfect drainage and moist soil. Sandy loam generously amended with organic matter is best. Give it full sun. Space plants 10 to 15 inches apart. Hardy to zone 2.

Care: Moderately easy. Mulch in summer and water over dry periods. Remove faded flowers to prolong the bloom period. Mulching over winter is recommended in harsh climates. There are few serious pests, but mildew and root rot have been reported. The clumps will start to degenerate in the third or fourth year, requiring division to restore vigor. This is also an excellent means of increase, and should be done in the spring.

Sedum spectabile
and hybrids
(Showy Stonecrop; Showy Sedum)
Stonecrop family. Native to China and Japan.

These mounded, 2-foot plants have fleshy, light green leaves topped with many flat clusters of flowers from August to frost. They are especially effective massed in the border, or in beds all to themselves.

The flowers are various shades of pink, rose, and white, turning to bronze as they mature and develop fruit in the fall. Individually they are tiny and produced in dense, flat-topped or hemispherical clusters 3 to 4 inches across, often covering the top of the plant. Most cultivars are attractive to butterflies. They bloom in early August to the middle of September. The bronze fruits are attractive well into frost.

The light green leaves often appear dusted with white, and are thick, fleshy, and rounded. Growing to about 3 inches across, they are arranged either oppositely or whorled against the succulent stems.

Clusters of many upright to spreading stems are densely clothed with leaves, each stem ending in a flat flower cluster. Neat and tidy, the overall form is mounded, growing 18 to 24 inches high. The foliage is clean and attractive all season.

The clumps will expand by producing new shoots on the outer ridges. In very rich soils they have a tendency to spread apart, revealing an open center. The showy sedum is a long-lived plant and is never invasive.

How to start: Nursery plants and divisions are best planted in spring. Stem cuttings root easily and should be made in summer. Seeds can be sown in late summer or mid-spring at 65°. Hybrids will not breed true from seed.

Where to plant: Sedums are not particular about soil as long as it is well drained. This group needs moist, richer soil than usually supposed for sedum and will grow in quite wet ones. Give the plants full sun; partial shade is best in hot climates. Space plants 12 to 18 inches apart. Hardy to zone 3.

Care: Easy. This sedum responds to adequate water. It has no serious pests. Although the plant can go many years without requiring division for rejuvenation, division is an excellent means of increase and is best done in spring.

Solidago canadensis 'Golden Baby'

Stachys byzantina with edging lobelia and *Achillea ptarmica* 'The Pearl'

Solidago hybrids
(Goldenrod)
Daisy family. While the parentage is uncertain, most are probably from Europe and the eastern United States.

Much successful hybridizing has resulted in outstanding golden yellow color on solid, easily grown plants.

Contrary to popular belief, goldenrod does not cause hay fever. The heavy, waxy pollen is insect-borne, and never travels on the wind. The insidious hay-fever-causing ragweeds (*Ambrosia* species) bloom at approximately the same time. No doubt this has led to blaming the more conspicuous, and innocent, goldenrod.

The flowers appear in various shades of yellow, from primrose and canary to dark gold. Individually they are tiny, but they are produced in great quantities in flat-topped clusters, or along pedicels held perpendicular to the stem. They bloom in August and September.

The medium green, lance-shape leaves are held tightly against the upright stems. The branching, upright or slightly spreading stems grow in clusters, 18 to 40 inches tall and generally in a vase shape.

Goldenrods are long-lived, restrained in growth, and never invasive. They slowly increase by sending up shoots along the outside perimeter of the clump.

How to start: Plant nursery plants or divisions either in spring or fall.

Where to plant: Goldenrods are quite adaptable to most any soil, although very wet or dry ones should be avoided. Give them full sun. Space plants 12 to 15 inches apart. Hardy to zone 3.

Care: Easy. The tallest varieties may require staking if grown in rich soils. The plant has no serious pests. It can go for years without requiring division for rejuvenation. To increase, divide in spring or late fall.

Stachys byzantina
(Lamb's Ear; Wooly Betony)
Mint family. Native to Turkey and Southwest Asia.

Lamb's ear is a low, tufted plant grown for its outstanding foliage. The leaves are densely wooly and intense silvery white in color. In the front of the border it makes an eye-catching accent, particularly on moonlit nights. And it is especially pleasing when combined with pastel shades of blue and pink flowers.

The flowers of lamb's ear are purplish white. Individually they are small, about ½ inch long, and arranged in whorls at the top of 4- to 6-inch spikes. They bloom from July through September, and are pleasant but not particularly showy. The plant is grown primarily for its foliage. ('Silver Carpet' is a nonflowering form.)

The leaves grow to an oblong or tonguelike shape 4 to 6 inches long. They are arranged in low radial clumps 6 to 12 inches high and often spread 24 inches wide. Lamb's ear can be quite long-lived, but is always neat and restrained in its growth. The clumps expand slowly, but after several years they begin to die out in the center, necessitating division.

Stachys officinalis

How to start: Nursery plants or division in spring are the usual methods, but this plant is easy to start from seed sown outdoors in mid-spring, or indoors in early spring at 65°. Germination usually takes less than a week.

Where to plant: The soil must have perfect drainage, and should be of only moderate fertility. Lamb's ear is prone to rotting in muggy, humid climates. Give it full sun. Space plants 10 to 15 inches apart. Hardy to zone 4.

Care: Moderately easy. Avoid overwatering. There are no serious pests. Divide after the fourth year to rejuvenate. Division is also an excellent means of increase.

Stokesia laevis

Thalictrum aquilegifolium
with tulips

Related species: *Stachys grandiflora* (Big Betony) is a taller, bushy plant with grayish-green leaves. It produces great quantities of bright purple flowers 1 inch long and gathered in whorls around tall spikes. They bloom in May and June. The flowers are beloved by bees. The plant grows best in partial shade.

S. officinalis is similar to big betony, but with smaller, less impressive flowers. It produces tall, whorled flower spikes of rosy purple in July and August. It is best in full sun and a dry soil.

Stokesia laevis
(Stokes' Aster)
Daisy family. Native to South Carolina south to Louisiana and Florida.

The flowers of this perennial resemble a cross between an aster and a pincushion flower. They are most effective when grown in small groups in the mixed border.

The flowers are lavender to silvery or dark blue, and sometimes pure white. Like a daisy, they have an outer single or double row of "petals," or, more accurately, ray florets, and a center of fuzzy-looking disc florets in the same color. They are produced singly at the ends of the stems, blooming in July and August.

The narrow, dark green, lance-shape leaves can grow to 8 inches long. Large basal clumps of leaves support many flower stalks. The plant grows 12 to 18

inches high. The Stokes' aster can be long-lived if the soil is perfectly drained in winter. The clumps often get crowded by the fourth year, requiring division.

How to start: The plant is easy to start from seed sown outdoors in April. Nursery plants or clump divisions can also be planted in the spring.

Where to plant: Stokes' aster is utterly intolerant of wet soil in winter, so sharp drainage is a must. Otherwise it is not too particular about soil. Give it full sun. Space plants 12 to 15 inches apart. Hardy to zone 6.

Care: Moderately difficult, being quite touchy about soggy soil in winter. Otherwise, it requires little special attention. There are no serious pests. Division is required about every 4 years to reduce crowding. Also a good means of increase, it is best performed in spring.

Thalictrum rochebrunianum
(Lavender Mist Meadowrue)
Buttercup family. Native to Japan.

These tall, airy plants have finely textured foliage topped with delicate sprays of lavender flowers. Growing 3 to 6 feet high or more, this meadowrue makes a splendid background.

The flowers are lavender-violet with bright yellow stamens. Individually they are minute and have no petals; the showy parts are the purplish sepals and yellow stamens. They appear in great quantities on open, misty panicles, blooming in July and August.

The very delicate, medium-green leaves often have a bluish cast. They

are compound with many small three-leaf leaflets. The tall, multibranched stems grow 3 to 6 feet, and sometimes taller. An open, lacy appearance belies strong stems that never require staking. The foliage effect is similar to that of maidenhair fern, with which the plant is often compared.

Thalictrum grows slowly and is long-lived. New divisions may take 2 or 3 seasons to achieve the effect desired.

How to start: Seeds should be sown outdoors in the fall. Fresh seed will germinate best. Seed can be sown in spring if given a 3- to 5-week period of pre-chilling in the refrigerator; but germination is often erratic. Nursery plants or divisions planted in spring are preferable, although fall plantings are usually successful with winter protection.

Where to plant: The plant prefers deep, rich, moist soil high in organic matter. Partial shade is best, but full sun is tolerated if the soil is kept moist. Space plants 24 inches apart. Hardy to zone 5.

Care: Moderately easy. Meadowrue appreciates abundant water. It has few serious pests, but powdery mildew and rust are occasionally reported. It is best to divide the plant about every fifth year to relieve crowding of the root mass. An excellent means of increase, this should be done either in spring or fall. Divisions planted·in fall should be mulched over winter.

Related species: *Thalictrum aquilegifolium* (Columbine Meadowrue). Fluffy, pinkish-purple flowers are effective from late May to early June on 3-foot stems. Rose and white varieties are also available. The grayish-green foliage resembles columbine in both texture and color. More widely grown than the above species, but smaller and less refined.

Thermopsis caroliniana

Tradescantia virginiana

Thermopsis caroliniana
(False Lupine)
Pea family. Native from North Carolina to Georgia.

Resembling a tall, slender yellow lupine, with its spikes of pealike flowers, thermopsis will withstand the hot, muggy weather of the Southeast. It is also easy and completely hardy elsewhere in the United States. Relatively unknown, it may be difficult to locate commercially.

The individual flowers are small and are gathered into 10- to 12-inch spikes atop erect stems. They bloom in June and early July.

The dark green leaves are divided into three leaflets. The plant forms clusters of rigidly upright stems clothed in leaves and tipped with flower spikes. It grows up to 4 feet tall and often spreads 3 feet wide.

False lupine is long-lived and restrained in growth. It seldom needs division. Early to appear and fast-growing in the spring, the foliage remains lush and dense all season long.

How to start: Easy to start from seed sown in late summer. Before sowing, soak the seeds in warm water or file the seed coats. The plant can also be started by nursery plants or from clump divisions planted in late summer.

Where to plant: Well-drained soil of poor to average fertility. Like most members of the pea family, root nodules "fix" nitrogen from the atmosphere; the false lupine almost never needs fertilizing, and soil that is excessively rich in nitrogen will promote yellowing of the leaves. Full sun is best, although it tolerates partial shade well. Space plants 24 to 40 inches apart. Hardy to zone 3.

Care: Easy. Some support probably will be necessary in windy areas. It has no serious pests. Division is rarely required for rejuvenation, which is fortunate, since division of old clumps is difficult because of the dense, deep roots. It is frequently unsuccessful, but if attempted, should be performed in late summer.

Tradescantia virginiana
(Spiderwort)
Spiderwort family. Native to the eastern United States.

Adaptable to many difficult situations, including infertile soil, deep shade, and boggy conditions, the spiderwort will provide colorful blooms over a long season. It can, however, have a tendency to sprawl and ramble through the garden when it is not restrained. Named cultivars are usually superior to the native species.

The flowers are usually bright purple, although many varieties have been selected that are white, blue, purple, pink, or red. The blossoms are composed of three petals, are about 1 inch wide, and last individually for only a day; however, they are produced in clusters at the ends of the stems and bloom over a long season, from June to September.

The deep green leaves are almost straplike, growing to 1 inch wide and as long as 15 inches. The lower portion of the leaf is wrapped around the stem, giving the plant the appearance of a coarse grass. The form is variable, but mostly upright, and the plant is from 18 to 36 inches high. The stems are angled at the joints. From midseason on, the plant will tend to sprawl into an open, tangled structure.

Spiderwort will spread enthusiastially by underground stems, and by aboveground stems that root where their joints contact the soil. It is long-lived, but requires frequent division to restrain its rampant growth.

How to start: The species is easy to start by seed sown in the spring, but best results will occur from fresh seed collected and sown in late summer. Germination takes about 2 weeks. Nursery plants or divisions of named cultivars should be planted in spring.

Where to plant: Spiderwort tolerates nearly any soil, but grows most vigorously in moist, rich ones, which should be avoided by gardeners desiring to restrain the plant. Give it full sun to deep shade. Space plants 15 to 30 inches apart. Native to moist soils in the eastern United States, it is hardy to zone 4.

Care: Easy, but it can be moderately difficult to restrain. The plant will look best with adequate water. If the stems flop badly in midsummer, they can be cut clear to the ground; the revived plant will flower again in the fall.

The plant has few serious pests, although several caterpillars have been reported. Botrytis blight may attack the blossoms.

Division is best performed every other year, and should be done every third or fourth year to restrain spreading. It is an excellent means of increase, and should be performed in the spring.

Trollius
'Orange Princess'

Veronica longifolia
'Blue Peter'

Trollius europaeus
and hybrids
(Common Globe Flower)
Buttercup family. Native to Europe and
arctic North America.

Globe flowers are leafy, bushy plants
that produce rounded, globular blossoms in many shades of yellow and orange. Blooming in late spring and early
summer, they are an excellent choice
for moist, heavy soil that most other
perennials abhor.

Flowers come in many shades of yellow and orange, according to variety.
They are 1 to 3 inches across and are
composed of five to fifteen showy sepals
in a rounded, ball-like mass that looks
as if it has never fully opened. The
flowers appear on the ends of long
stems in May and June.

The dark green leaves are deeply divided into three to five lobes and have
a medium texture. The basal leaves
have stalks, and are larger and more
dense than the stem leaves, whose bottom portions wrap around the stems.
The stems grow 1 to 3 feet tall, depending upon variety, and in upright
clusters, creating bushy, rounded
masses. Foliage is attractive all season.

Globe flowers are long-lived and restrained in growth. The clumps gradually expand by sending up new shoots
on the outside perimeter of the crown.

How to start: Planting divisions in
late summer is the best method. Plants
can also be started from seed first frozen for 2 days in the refrigerator, then
sown outdoors in late summer. Fresh
seed germinates well in 6 or 7 weeks.
Old seed may take 2 years or more to
sprout.

Where to plant: Fertile, very moist
soil high in organic matter is best, but
avoid boggy conditions. While prefer-

ring partial shade, globe flowers tolerate full sun if the soil is kept moist.
Space plants 12 inches apart. Hardy to
zone 3.

Care: Easy in moist soil. Remove
faded flowers to prolong the bloom
period. Keep well watered, as these
plants must never dry out. They have
no serious pests. The plant usually requires division every 5 years or so to
reduce crowding, but if necessary can
survive much longer without disturbance. An excellent means of increase,
division should be done in late summer.

Veronica
hybrids
(Speedwell)
Snapdragon family. Of diverse hybrid
origin; parents are generally native to
Europe and Asia.

The colorful spikes of veronica make
quite a show in July and August. Many
cultivars are available, and most are selected from crosses between *Veronica
longifolia* and *V. spicata*. Several other
species are of interest, also, and they
are noted in this entry.

The flowers are usually blue, although varieties are available in pink,
purple, and white. Individually they are
small and gathered into dense, narrow
spikes at the ends of the branches.
They bloom in late June through the
middle of August.

The light green leaves sometimes
have a grayish cast, are lance-shape,
and about 2 inches long. Of medium
texture, they are held opposite one another on the upright stems. The plant
produces bushy clusters of stems that
can be either branched or unbranched.
Varieties range in size from 12 to 30
inches tall, although most grow to
around 18 inches.

Most varieties are long-lived and
fairly restrained in growth. The clumps
enlarge by sending up many new
shoots at the perimeter.

How to start: Named varieties should
be started by divisions planted in spring
or fall. You can sow seed outdoors in
the spring, but considerable variation
will result from hybrid seed.

Where to plant: The soil should not
be overly fertile, but it must be well
drained. Full sun is best, but the plant
tolerates partial shade. Space plants 12
to 18 inches apart. Hardy to zone 4.

Care: Moderately easy. Removing
faded flowers will prolong the bloom
season. Downy mildew and leaf spot
can be serious problems, especially in
humid areas. If these diseases are likely,
protect the plants with a fungicide. Division probably is necessary every 4
years for the best appearance of most
varieties. It is an excellent means of increase, and should be done either in
the spring or fall.

Related species and varieties: *Veronica incana* (Wooly Speedwell) has white,
furry leaves on 12- to 18-inch stems.
The foliage contrasts well with the pale
blue flower spikes in June and July.
This plant must have excellent drainage
to survive wet winters.

V. latifolia 'Crater Lake Blue', formerly called *V. teucrium*, has bright blue
flowers over a long season, nearly all
summer long. It grows to 18 inches
with a tangled, much-branched habit of
growth.

V. longifolia (Clump Speedwell) bears
light blue flowers on 12-inch plants
from July through August.

V. spicata (Spike Speedwell) is similar
to the above, growing 18 inches tall
with many branches. The flower spikes
are usually shorter, but are very densely
produced.